LALLY KATZ is one of Australia's most performed playwrights. Her plays display a rare and original voice for the stage in works including *The Eisteddfod*, *The Black Swan of Trespass*, *A Golem Story*, *Starchaser* and *Neighbourhood Watch*. Lally started her career making theatre with director Chris Kohn at Stuck Pigs Squealing wherever they could find an audience and created a strong reputation for their work, winning the 2005 Producer's Choice Award at the International Fringe Festival in New York. Lally has developed new work with the National Theatre in England, was a writer in residence at Melbourne University, won the British Council's Realise Your Dream Award and received a Churchill Fellowship. *Goodbye Vaudeville Charlie Mudd* won the Victorian Premier's Award in 2009 and other work has variously won Green Room awards, Sydney Theatre awards and the RE Ross Trust Award.

From left: Christen O'Leary as Maude, Alex Menglet as Allarkini, Julia Zemiro as Ethylyn, Jim Russell as Charlie and Matt Wilson as Knuckles in the 2009 Arena Theatre Company and Malthouse Theatre production of Goodbye Vaudeville Charlie Mudd *at the Malthouse Theatre, Melbourne. (Photo: Jeff Busby)*

Goodbye Vaudeville Charlie Mudd

Written by **Lally Katz**
Concept by **Chris Kohn**

&

RETURN TO EARTH

Written by **Lally Katz**

CURRENCY PLAYS

First published in 2012
by Currency Press Pty Ltd,
PO Box 2287, Strawberry Hills, NSW, 2012, Australia
enquiries@currency.com.au
www.currency.com.au

Copyright: Introduction © Chris Mead, 2012; *Goodbye Vaudeville Charlie Mudd* © Lally Katz and Chris Kohn, 2012; *Return to Earth* © Lally Katz, 2012.

COPYING FOR EDUCATIONAL PURPOSES

The Australian *Copyright Act 1968* (Act) allows a maximum of one chapter or 10% of this book, whichever is the greater, to be copied by any educational institution for its educational purposes provided that that educational institution (or the body that administers it) has given a remuneration notice to Copyright Agency Limited (CAL) under the Act. For details of the CAL licence for educational institutions contact CAL, Level 15, 233 Castlereagh Street, Sydney, NSW, 2000; tel: within Australia 1800 066 844 toll free; outside Australia +61 2 9394 7600; fax: +61 2 9394 7601; email: info@copyright.com.au

COPYING FOR OTHER PURPOSES

Except as permitted under the Act, for example a fair dealing for the purposes of study, research, criticism or review, no part of this book may be reproduced, stored in a retrieval system, or transmitted in any form or by any means without prior written permission. All enquiries should be made to the publisher at the address above. Any performance or public reading of *Goodbye Vaudeville Charlie Mudd* or *Return to Earth* is forbidden unless a licence has been received from the author or the author's agent. The purchase of this book in no way gives the purchaser the right to perform the plays in public, whether by means of a staged production or a reading. All applications for public performance should be addressed to The Yellow Agency, PO Box 164 Erskineville NSW 2043; tel: +61 2 8090 4421; email: contact@theyellowagency.com.au

NATIONAL LIBRARY OF AUSTRALIA CIP DATA

    Author: Katz, Lally.
    Title: Goodbye Vaudeville Charlie Mudd & Return to Earth / by Lally Katz.
    ISBN: 9780868199382 (pbk.)
    Subjects: Australian drama—21st century.
    Other Authors/Contributors:
                        Kohn, Chris.
    Dewey Number: A822.4

Goobye Vaudeville Charlie Mudd & Return to Earth was created with assistance from the Commonwealth Government through the Australia Council, its arts funding and advisory body.

Contents

Introduction	
Chris Mead	*vii*
GOODBYE VAUDEVILLE CHARLIE MUDD	1
Prologue	5
Act One	6
Act Two	32
Act Three	74
RETURN TO EARTH	77
Act One	83
Act Two	114
Act Three	125

Typeset by Dean Nottle for Currency Press.
Cover design by Katy Wall for Currency Press.
Front cover shows the 2011 Melbourne Theatre Company production of *Return to Earth*. Back cover shows Alex Menglet as Allarkini and Christen O'Leary as Maude in the 2009 Arena Theatre Company and Malthouse Theatre production of *Goodbye Vaudeville Charlie Mudd* at the Malthouse Theatre, Melbourne.
(Photos: Jeff Busby)

Currency Press acknowledges the Traditional Owners of the Country on which we live and work. We pay our respects to all Aboriginal and Torres Strait Islander Elders, past and present.

Eloise Mignon as Alice and Anthony Ahern as Theo in the 2011 Melbourne Theatre Company production of Return to Earth. *(Photo Jeff Busby)*

INTRODUCTION

For those lucky enough to have met Lally Katz they will most certainly agree that one of her most distinctive qualities is her laugh. It is broad, explosive, generous and betrays her enormous optimism, quick intelligence, curiosity and abandon. There is nothing mocking in her laugh—rather it reveals her openness to the world and, most particularly, to incongruity, the lateral and the abstract. And it's not because she likes a laugh that her plays end up being funny—there is neither always nor already a direct equivalence between a writer's life and their work.* Her laugh—dangerous and contagious as it is—is a clue to better understanding her work.

That said, and it is worth making it plain, Lally's plays are funny—and they have been since she began writing. This made her, and her work, remarkable from the beginning. Not many emerging writers gravitate towards comedy, or even comedy drama. Most prefer, instead, the bold statements, the unalloyed seriousness and the emotional contours of drama—indeed most new playwrights pen solipsistic, naturalistic family-dilemma plays—but Lally unself-consciously works with comedy, with the fantastical and the absurd, with comedy as a form. Her plays aren't lightweight crowd-pleasers with happy endings that reinforce social norms and humiliate the vulnerable (as some more formulaic comedies do) rather she uses humour to cut deep into difficult emotional terrain—and she even uses comedy to question the form itself.

Her plays contain gags and extravagant, hilarious, imaginative landscapes, madcap quests and delirious, delusional, always charming characters, but her plays also actively ask more troubling and more interrogative meta-theatrical questions around the notion of what is appropriately funny; and further, what humour does to us and to an

---

* That said though, Lally more than most playwrights blurs the line between herself and her work: in many of her plays Lally Katz appears as a voice or a character; and the character Catta, who bears many resemblances to Lally, has so far cropped up in four of her plays.

audience's reception of story—what should we be laughing at? Indeed, what are we laughing at? In *Goodbye Vaudeville Charlie Mudd* a varied troupe of entertainers fail at their jobs and ultimately uncover a series of murders ruining the title character; and in *Return to Earth* a disturbed young woman is unlucky in love, upsets her parents and fails to help her dying niece. Neither of these stories seem either funny or fit for comedy, yet Lally uses comic set-ups and consistent surprises to dramatise real stories of loss and reckoning.

Before looking in more detail at how the two plays in this volume function it is worth noting two more remarkable things about Lally Katz—the first is the way she blazed a trail for a generation of playwrights. When I first became involved in Australian theatre in the 1990s the play script and the lone writer in the garret were both viewed with some suspicion and perhaps even disdain. Few Australian plays were produced and the pathway for playwrights was not at all clear. Lally's response—rather than to get cross and rail and rant and keep writing in her garret—was to find collaborators and simply get on with it. It is one of the great truisms of theatre that it is a collaborative medium—a truism often especially tricky for playwrights to embrace— and while she pursued a singular vision she also found like-minded artists up to the formal and practical challenges of her imagination, artists who could, and did, extend her talent and enhance her vision. Indeed, one of the great recent collaborations of Melbourne's independent theatre scene—which has an impressive history of writer/ director collaborations including the Keene-Taylor Project and Ranters Theatre's Cortese brothers—was that between Lally and Chris Kohn and their company Stuck Pigs Squealing. They created astonishing and multi-award-winning works for the theatre. That it inspired other playwrights is an understatement.

My office is full of piles and piles of unproduced plays, but because Lally got her hands dirty in small, bespoke theatres in Melbourne and Sydney her plays never remained in such a pile for long. She instead watched as her words leapt off the page and bounced around an audience. This is one of the other remarkable things about Lally—she got to know the possibilities and challenges of the medium of theatre on the job, that is, she learnt how to 'wright' theatre by doing it. At a time when the term post-dramatic theatre was gaining currency, 'Australianness' in theatre was increasingly rejected as a parochial straightjacket, starkness and austerity of dialogue and design were *de rigueur*, and anti-humanist, de-humanised characters featured, she wrote dense but volatile, baroque yet domestic, dialogue-driven, funny, big-hearted plays steeped in questions of belonging and cultural identity. Her characters were fragile but her worlds were robust; and she made the most of theatre's plasticity, that is, the flexibility and dynamism of its melding of truth and fictive power. Lally revelled in theatre's schizophrenia—framing and re-framing questions of a character's truth in fantastic worlds of absurd struggles and everyday but impossible, implausible obstacles. Death often loomed large and the disintegration of a character, of character as a coherent principle, was always very close, almost a given. That Lally managed such complex encounters and difficult thematics with such buoyancy is testament to her growing understanding, and love, of the audience, her use of humour, her deep experience of the 'alive-ness' of theatre and of the power and limits of language, coupled with an innate sympathy for the inevitability of lives lived topsy-turvy.

That she was attracted to an entity as explicitly theatrical as vaudeville makes for a rewarding theatrical experience in *Goodbye Vaudeville Charlie Mudd*. Plays based on research can sometimes be arch, dry or overburdened by facts but Lally and Chris' Creative Fellowship at the State Library of Victoria yielded a play that met the form of vaudeville head-on, it is funny and peculiar. It is rich in veracity for period acts, but also in veracity for vaudeville's playful duplicity—in this fictional Melbourne on the Swanston River the magic is real, minstrel blackface is 'skin', racism and sexism are unflinchingly commonplace and in Charlie Mudd's Castle the fantastic is both possible and necessary, performers need acts after all. Music hall and vaudeville (their differences are important) were common in Victorian and Edwardian Australia and Lally connects with the latter's formal variety—the ridiculous, the all-too-human and the hyperbolic all-jostling for attention, not to mention the singing, acrobatics, dumb shows, ventriloquism and dancing—as a vehicle to frame a more complex story about the dangers of the seeming and the real. She has not only crafted a strange story of particular characters' ignominy and despair but she places them in this vehicle, this structure, this machine—Mudd's Castle, vaudeville the form, the play itself—which encases and imprisons them, a manufactory that feeds the audience's ghoulish desire to consume the weak and the extraordinary. It is both a play about pain and cruel desire, and about our need for laughter, the palaces we build for it, and its human cost, for the characters, and for us. As Bones comments: 'The magic of the minstrel show will never die. So long as we feed it with our own blood—feed it with our lives…' (p.31)

(As a work for the theatre *Goodbye Vaudeville Charlie Mudd* poses powerful questions relating to its internal machinations—mostly clustered around the conundrum: enjoy the artifice, it's real, even deadly. The observations are rich and profound—how do we hold time at bay? Does humour always betray pain? Is love always a haunting? Can we shut out the world while still living in it? There is something especially provocative, however, in the way the three acts work across this play. There are character questions: what happens to Violet between Acts One and Two? Does knowing the characters on and off-stage increase or obfuscate our understanding of them? What happened to the other Ethelyns? And what is happening to this one? Are they all the walking dead? There are also interesting questions here about duration and the way we experience time in performance: we witness an actual show, and then the hustle and bustle before a show, and then the overflowing of mud and debris as Charlie's time is literally up. There is something fascinating too about the restlessness of the form—we are never fixed in time or place—it seems to happen over a couple of nights and in the one place, but we are outside the show, then inside their world, then inside characters' heads. Can the story stay in its expected narrative banks or will it overflow, ensuring chaos and story bedlam? Like all good plays this one keeps us guessing and is a *wunderkammer* of delights, problems and possibilities, perceived and real.)

Return to Earth is Lally's most significant play to date. What I love about this play is that the dilemmas are so painful, so real, so well-observed, yet so particular and so strange. It too is a funny play; awkward, even prosaic at times, mundane, edging on the whimsical but ultimately it is lyrical and profound. Alice's obfuscations are infuriating for us and for those closest to her, but one can't help but be utterly charmed by her honesty, openness and lack of guile. There is poignancy here, tenderness and yet darkness too as they face a welter of dreadful decisions. The moment a young person moves from transparency to opacity, from childhood to adulthood is fraught, often littered with casualties—it is a period of intense loss and confusion, something Lally captures prismatically, precisely and with real emotional truth.

Return to Earth reveals her talent for writing persuasive naturalism married here with her distinctive zany, multivalent and anarchic style. This is a play about the struggle to be in the world—a world of brutality and pitiless chance—but it is also a play about how to be a Lally Katz play in the world. Alice is sure where she is but not at all sure about where she finds herself; and the play, while naturalistic, contains shards of the strange and the extraordinary. Alice and Lally both seem to ask: How do you remain true to the voice/s, and the worlds in your head, without, ignoring, imperilling, lying to or maddening those around you? Or abandoning what has made you distinctively you? And just to make matters even more multiple, Lally's real parents live in Tathra, the setting of the play, and the place to which Alice/Erika the runaway daughter has returned. There is an ontological and absurd project at work here, but also a simpler one of the balance to be found between conformity and authenticity, ordinariness and beauty, tranquillity and contingency, living and dying, the many and the one. *Return to Earth* is a play to be savoured and enjoyed and as the French philosopher Henri Bergson, and the American essayist and children's author E.B. White observed, comedy can be studied and splayed but such effort ultimately does no justice to it as a living, dynamic system. Read, perform and enjoy *Return to Earth*—but be warned its tone is difficult to capture. This is a play that might seem freewheeling and light-hearted, but is actually deeply serious and performatively precarious, almost vertiginously so. Good comedy, good theatre, is like that.

The production of laughter is difficult and delicate (ask any actor, director, playwright, comedian, impromptu speaker and so on) but it emerges as a result of complex interconnections across the limbic system, an ancient, deep and highly evolved part of the brain crucial for memory, sensory perception, self-preservation, fear, anger and arousal. While scientists tell us this, for most of us, it remains elusive, accidental and perplexing. Laughter, however, is lodged deep within Lally's work—her plays make allusive, lateral connections, dredge up ancient memories, are about the will to survive and the absurd situations we too often find ourselves in: can we go on? We must go on. Australians have perfected our own version of gallows humour and we see it in abundance in these two plays. The shared experience of the liminal and the terrifying can be funny and transformative, an escape from despair, and we are all the better for undergoing it together. Lally writes plays that disarm, unsettle but enlighten, plays where innocence is valued, where pain is real but laughter echoes, winning us over despite the suffering because here is insight, kindness and vulnerability. Lally deploys humour to make the familiar strange and the strange familiar, disturbing the orthodox, the pompous and the intractable. This is playwriting at its most disruptive, irruptive, searching and subversive. Lally Katz plays are eccentric, silly, vulgar, playful, odd and strangely recognisable and they smuggle through unique and piercing investigations into the mystery, and wonder, of being.

Chris Mead

Chris Mead is Literary Director of Melbourne Theatre Company. He was the founding artistic director of Playwriting Australia. His most recent directing credits include *Quack* by Ian Wilding and *The Modern International Dead* by Damien Millar.

Goodbye Vaudeville Charlie Mudd

Written by **Lally Katz**
Concept by **Chris Kohn**

Dedicated to Stephen Armstrong and Michael Kantor

Goodbye Vaudeville Charlie Mudd was first produced by the Malthouse Theatre and Arena Theatre Company at the Beckett Theatre, Malthouse, Melbourne, on 11 March 2009, with the following cast:

CHARLIE MUDD	JIM RUSSELL
VIOLET/ETHEYLN	JULIA ZEMIRO
BONES	MARK JONES
MAUDE AND HER DUMMY DORIS	CHRISTEN O'LEARY
ALLARKINI	ALEX MENGLET
KNUCKLES	MATT WILSON

Director, Chris Kohn
Assistant Director, Christian Leavesley
Dramaturg, Maryanne Lynch
Designer, Jonathan Oxlade
Lighting Designer, Richard Vabre
Sound Designer, Jethro Woodward
Composer, Mark Jones
Song Lyrics, Lally Katz and Chris Kohn
Illussionist, Lawrence Leung

Based in Melbourne, Arena Theatre Company has a 46-year history of creating original theatre works for young people, aged 5–25, and their families. Arena's artistic vision is founded on the belief that theatre creates a space that is surprising, alive, fertile, explosive, dangerous and inspiring. Arena's diverse program includes new commissions of in-theatre work, large-scale interactive installation, engagement processes and access programs for emerging artists. More information can be found at www.arenatheatre.com.au

CHARACTERS

CHARLIE MUDD, the owner and interlocutor of Mudd's Vaudeville Castle

VIOLET / ETHELYN RARITY, singer, dancer, butterfly impersonator—the same actor plays both roles

BONES, theatre musician and black-face minstrel

MAUDE, ventriloquist

DORIS, Maude's foul-mouthed dummy

ALLARKINI, magician

KNUCKLES, Charlie's mute, acrobatic brother

All of these characters have somehow come to live their vaudeville 'act'.

SETTING

A theatre. Helpful if it can look a vaudeville theatre from around 1914.

In the first act of the play, the action takes place in front of the drawn curtain, and then upon the stage in real time. In the second half, after interval, the action takes place backstage, onstage and finally in front of the curtain again.

ACKNOWLEDGMENTS

Thank you to everyone at the Malthouse Theatre, Frank Van Straten, Dianne Reilly and the State Library of Victoria, Malcolm Robertson and the performers who participated in the developments of the show.

PROLOGUE

The very beginning. With the red curtain closed. In black-face,
BONES *speaks, to what we must assume is us, the audience.*

BONES: Master Manuel Arni—juvenile conductor. Atlas—athletic champion of England and cycle whiz. Bert Bayden—coon comedian. Bob Bell—dwarf comique. Little Edna, Champion Club and Axe Swinger of Australasia, Daly and O'Brien—'Tanglefoot' dancers, Miss Minnie Kaufman—the trick cyclist, The Royal Banzai and Madame De Dio with her prismatic dancing. No-one remembers them, folks. Only you know you've heard their names. Some might say dey was 'buried in history'. But tain't history dat buried 'em. Surely, it were history dat forgot 'em. I won't argue that. But de only ting dat buried 'em was tomorrow. I want to invite you folks into de night before tomorrow. It's the year 1914. Just before the Great War started up. And it be the end of what were known as the 'Edwardian Summer'. The end of a time when alls you had to do were dream to make it so. And here we is. In Charlie Mudd's Vaudeville Castle. On the edge of Swanston River. You ever heard the legend of Swanston River? Hardly no-one know now where it be. 'Casionally someone, half sleepin', stumble 'pon us when they miss theys tram. When they falls off their bicycly. When theys steps, not lookin' onto the street and their shoe fill up with water.

He starts to play the piano as he speaks.

Maude Adle. Ventriloquist, singer and musical paper tearer. Knuckles. Acrobat and domestic balancer. Allarkini. Magician and man of mystery. Ethelyn Rarity, insect impersonator and singer of dramatic arias. Mr Bones. End man. Charlie Mudd. Interlocutor, hat thrower, equestrian sensation, owner of Mudd's Castle. We is glad you is come here. You is come down by Swanston River. Down here with us, on the night before tomorrow.

ACT ONE

SCENE ONE

A light comes up. In front of the red curtain.
The red curtain is closed. We can't see behind it.
In front of it, on the long sliver of stage available, a young woman, carrying a small travelling case, is standing. VIOLET. *We do not see her arrive.*
She is very simply, there.
She looks around. There is no-one else there.

VIOLET: Hello? Hello? Hello, Mr Mudd?

> BONES *stares out with his eyes big, his mouth a little 'o'. His eyes sweep over the stage in front of the curtain. They rest on* VIOLET. *And then depart nervously to the audience seats.*

BONES: Is it jus' you alone there?
VIOLET: Yes. Were you expecting someone else? I don't have a partner in my act.
BONES: Well, there is one other person we's 'xpectin'—but you must be the new girl…
VIOLET: Violet! And you must be Mister…
BONES: Bones. You is late.
VIOLET: I'm dreadfully sorry for my tardiness, Mr Bones. I must confess I had the most difficult time in finding the theatre. You see the directions I had said it was on Swanston River. But that's no river. It's barely even a puddle.
BONES: All but dried up in the drought. Allow me to take your belongings now, Miss Violet.
VIOLET: Oh, no—you're too kind. I'll take them. Where shall I go?
BONES: Mr Charlie would wants that I assist you, Miss Violet.

> *He takes the case from her, which she carried with ease—but he drops suddenly with the weight of it, even though it appears to be quite small.*

He rights himself. And they continue on.

We'll give you the dressin' table that says Ethelyn Rarity. You'll see, it's the prettiest one. The very prettiest… Tablecloth an' everythin'.

VIOLET: Oh, I don't want to take anyone's place.

BONES: But that's what you're here for, Miss Violet. Miss Ethelyn Rarity ain't never comin' back.

They walk along beside the curtain.

Have to be quick, ain't much time for a tour. Them folks'll be arrivin' real soon. And tonight is a real special night.

VIOLET: What's so special about tonight?

BONES: Tonight we's got a very important guest comin'—a man thats could change the whole future of this theatre. Now back to the tour. Right here is the curtain. When them audiences come in, we's opens the curtain right up. An' when they is going, well we closes it again.

VIOLET: Tell me, Mr Bones, does it take a terribly long time for you to apply your make-up before each performance?

BONES: Make-up?

VIOLET: I'm sorry—the cork, does it take an awfully long time to apply?

BONES: I'm sorry, Miss Violet. You done lost me there.

He seems to have no idea what she is talking about. They come to the end of the curtain. There is a door there.

VIOLET: Mr Bones, where does this door lead to?

BONES: It lead to offstage.

VIOLET: Where's that?

BONES: It ain't nowhere.

VIOLET goes to touch the doorknob. Just as her fingertips reach it BONES speaks out suddenly:

Don't touch please, Miss Violet. You mustn't never touch that door, y'hear!

There is an awkward silence as VIOLET's suspended hand slowly falls back down to her side.

VIOLET: Why not?

A man, dark and mysterious, has slipped through the curtain. He is smiling sarcastically. ALLARKINI.

ALLARKINI: Indeed, why not? Why not? Why must Ethelyn never touch the door? Why? Why? Why?

He peers deep and close into her face, holding it with his hand, almost as if it were a specimen.

This one is different.

VIOLET *is transfixed by* ALLARKINI *holding her face and peering right in.*

Yes. To know certain. This is different kind of Ethelyn.

He lets go of her face and turns to BONES.

Where is Mudd?

BONES: Mr Charlie is behind the curtain.

ALLARKINI: Perhaps hiding in the fold. [*He looks once more at* VIOLET.] Poor Ethelyn. Poor, poor Ethelyn.

ALLARKINI *disappears into the curtain.*

VIOLET: Mr Bones, why did he call me Ethelyn? Did he mistake me for her?

BONES: It be the rule, Miss Violet.

VIOLET: The rule?

BONES: Well, Ms Violet, it's been so many names for Master Charlie to remember.

VIOLET: I see.

BONES: So he will call you by Ms Ethelyn's name. And his rule is all the artists they calls you by it too.

VIOLET: How many of these girls—these girls like me… how many have there been since Ethelyn… uh…

BONES: One day them folks'll gather back into Mudd's Castle, fill up the stalls—them faraway angel faces that floats up there in the seats o' the gods. Back again.

VIOLET: And until then my name is Ethelyn…

KNUCKLES *somersaults in. He stops at* VIOLET*'s feet. He looks up and leans his chin on his hand and smiles at her.*

Hi there! I'm Violet.

KNUCKLES *looks confused.*

Oh. I—I am Ethelyn. And who are you?

KNUCKLES *takes her hands in his, looks up at her sweetly and then raps her knuckles hard.*

Ouch!

KNUCKLES *then somersaults back underneath the curtain.*

BONES: Boss's brother. He never did get on too well with Miss Ethelyn.
VIOLET: Can't he talk?
BONES: Poor Knuckles be simple and mute. If it weren't for Master Charlie, Knuckles would have died on the street.

A female voice from behind the curtain:

DORIS: Here we go then.

A different sounding female voice speaks back:

MAUDE: Now, Doris… behave.
DORIS: She's already met the others.
MAUDE: All of them? Did she meet… him?
DORIS: He touched her.
MAUDE: He touched her?
DORIS: Right in the face.
MAUDE: On the face?!

MAUDE *and her dummy* DORIS *burst out from behind the red curtain.*

Hello, new Ethelyn.
DORIS: She looks hungry for it.
MAUDE: Maybe she's just missed lunch. Have you had all your meals today, new Ethelyn?
VIOLET: Yes…
DORIS: I'll bet she's looking for dessert.
MAUDE: Doris, she's probably just nervous. Everyone looks peculiar when they're nervous. You mustn't be so quick to judge, Doris. I'm sure she's a very nice girl who would never ever in her wildest dreams imagine having an illicit… union of any kind…
DORIS: Not if she's anything like the last one.
VIOLET: Listen here, I'm not anyone or like anyone other than myself— My name is—
DORIS: Forget it, kid. We know who you are. You're Ethelyn. The star of our show and the apple of our boss's eye.

VIOLET: I don't know what you're talking about. I haven't so much as met Mr Mudd yet.

DORIS: Not to mention the apple of some other eyes…

MAUDE: Some sweet, dark eyes… Don't, Doris—they're only ideas—that's all they are—ideas!

They disappear behind the curtain.

VIOLET: Where is Mr Mudd? I must speak to him—

BONES: You will have to wait on that.

VIOLET: No, really, it's very important that I see him now.

BONES: They is arrivin'.

VIOLET: Who? Who's arriving?

BONES: Why… the audience of course.

VIOLET: I must see Mr Mudd—it's of the most vital importance—it's to do with my act—

BONES: But there ain't no time, Miss Ethelyn. No time at all.

VIOLET: But what am I to do?

BONES: Alls you need is in dis book.

He hands her a kind of script/instruction manual.

SCENE TWO

The red curtain opens. And there's a feeling of power, excitement, like something's arriving or on the cusp of arriving. Like when later on how the movie credits blast onto the screen. And there's some kind of sadness too.

When the curtain opens, everyone else is in position. VIOLET *is left, standing in the middle of the stage.*

The others are all frozen in positions of their acts.

VIOLET *looks around at the others who are all completely still, including even* BONES, *at his piano.*

VIOLET *quickly assumes a pose. But it's awkward.*

A spotlight shines on CHARLIE. *Before he realises that it is on him, he whispers loudly to* BONES, *as he peers out into the audience:*

CHARLIE: Is he here?! Is he here?! [*He sees* VIOLET.] The new Ethelyn… she needs her costume—

And then he realises that the spotlight is on him. He begins to perform.

Hello and welcome, my friends. I'm Charlie Mudd, the owner and interlocutor of Mudd's Vaudeville Castle. I'm so pleased you could join us. On our little picnic here on the banks of Swanston River.

He begins to sing the '1914' song:

> Welcome, yes welcome, to 1914
> It's great to be living here in 1914,
> The people are peaceful, the economy's strong
> There's nothing that could possibly go wrong
> 1914, 1914…

The music continues, as CHARLIE *speaks to the audience.*

Welcome, ladies and gentlemen, to our minstrel show tonight. We all sure do hope you enjoy it. Progress! Some folks try an' hide from it. But here it is! You see it? Sitting up behind the wheel of an automobile. Biting at our heels with the teeth of time…

No-one on stage hears him. He says again, pointedly:

Biting at our heels with the teeth of time.

The performers remember and all show their ankle watches— a big fashion of the time.

Don't forget, ankle watches are sold in the foyer at half-time. Time. Sometimes it's soaring above us in the sky.

He goes back to the song. The others join in.

        Aeroplanes
ALL: We've got aeroplanes
        Zipping back and forth through the sky
CHARLIE: Pretty soon, we'll fly right up to the moon
ALL: And after that we'll fly right back by mid-afternoon
CHARLIE: It's not a case of bluffing to assert there's nothing we can't achieve
ALL: And all the wowsers who espouse hard times ahead are being naïve.
DORIS: What a freakin' blast!
CHARLIE: Welcome, yes welcome, to 1914

It's great to be living here in 1914
The people are peaceful, the economy's strong
There's nothing that could possibly go wrong
1914, 1914...

He speaks to the audience as they begin to pretend they're picnicking.

It's a beautiful sunny day, folks. Not a drop of rain in the sky. Of course that's no surprise. There hasn't been rain in an eternity. But what a perfect day for a picnic! Oh—and look who's joined us! There's Maude the ventriloquist and her little dummy Doris. What have you got for us in your picnic basket, girls?

MAUDE: Well, sandwiches—
DORIS: I'll be the meat.
MAUDE: Sausages.
DORIS: [*to the audience*] Now she's talking about you, boys!
MAUDE: Sticky buns...
DORIS: I've got 'em already!
CHARLIE: And who's that young chap, making all the tomfoolery by the water? Why, it's Knuckles! Ladies and gentlemen, let me introduce you to the greatest act of balance on any stage, anywhere. My own brother, Knuckles.

KNUCKLES does a magnificent balancing trick. CHARLIE *continues to sing.*

I don't know if you've noticed
I can't say if you've seen
The world today, in many ways
Is not all that it seems
I saw a Jewish man lend money for no interest at all
I saw a Scottish man as sober as a child
I saw a nigger, as I sniggered, kiss a lady and couldn't figure
If the lady wasn't just a dapper man in flapper clothes
That's how it goes
Welcome, yes welcome, to 1914
It's great to be living here in 1914
The people are peaceful, the economy's strong
There's nothing that could possibly go wrong...

BONES *plays a special piano solo.*

And right there by the watermelon is Mr Bones. Our favourite coon. [*To* BONES] Where did you learn that little number, Mr Bones?

BONES: It ain't nothin', Boss, just a song from the cotton fields I used to hum when I was nappin'.

CHARLIE: Well, I hope you're not thinking of napping tonight you lazy good-for-nothing! We've got quite a show ahead!

BONES *joins him in the song.*

Electric lamps

BONES: We've electric lamps, that burn all night and blaze like the sun

MAUDE: An incredible range of new remedies

DORIS: It can't be long before we've conquered every disease

ALLARKINI: And all the while, we'll keep on smiling, grinning while we're singing this song

ALL: You must agree that history will show the pessimists were all wrong

The song ends.

CHARLIE: Allarkini—our magician—where are you? Oh, skulking in the shadows of the trees. Such befitting picnic behaviour for a man of mystery.

ALLARKINI *is looking for something in the set by the backdrop. Looking for clues. He turns, glares at* CHARLIE, *but then speaks to the audience.*

ALLARKINI: Magic is to be found by those ones chosen to be finders. Sometimes the most obvious place is the most of hidden. But I, the Great Allarkini, vill to find!

There is a moment of awkwardness.

CHARLIE: Mmm... yes.

And then he snaps back into the act.

And last, but by never least, we're joined by our leading lady, Ethelyn Rarity. Here she is, you must know, Ethelyn... that you're everyone's darling.

VIOLET, *has meanwhile been trying desperately to keep up with the act.*

VIOLET: Thank you…
DORIS: It ain't a compliment.
CHARLIE: Tell us, Ethelyn, what will you delight us with on our picnic by the river?

> VIOLET *looks extremely nervous. She doesn't know what to say. The others all watch.*
>
> VIOLET *swallows and says:*

VIOLET: I—I do have a small act prepared…
CHARLIE: Do you hear that, ladies and gentlemen? Ethelyn has a small act prepared! Aren't we the lucky picnickers. Anything else?
VIOLET: A dance? You can expect to see a dance?
CHARLIE: Wonderful. And anything else?
VIOLET: I… I don't know, Mr Mudd.
CHARLIE: Well, come on, darling, you must have more than that.
VIOLET: I can't find my place!
DORIS: This one's worse that the last one.
MAUDE: Doris, give her time.
VIOLET: I wasn't expecting an audience!

They all laugh.

BONES: Should we get another one, Boss?
ALLARKINI: We must to start again.

> *And then* VIOLET *begins to sing. It is like her song comes from somewhere else.*

VIOLET: Oh, Swanston River,
    Deliver me back her
    I've nothin' but tomorrow
    And the sun don't shine down there

> *The others all stop, but* VIOLET *sings again, loudly:*

EVERYONE: And the sun don't shine down there…

> *They all look at her. There is an awkward pause. Everyone else takes the act back to the '1914' song.*

CHARLIE: Welcome, yes welcome, to 1914
    The happiest year that we've ever seen
    As long as everybody keeps on singing this song

> There is nothing that could possibly go wrong
> Welcome, yes welcome, to 1914
> The happiest year that we've ever seen
> As long as everybody keeps on singing this song
> There's nothing that could possibly go wrong
> No absolutely nothing could go wrong

ALLARKINI: Already quite a few things have gone wrong
CHARLIE: But nothing more could possibly go wrong
ALL: No nothing more could possibly go wrong
> Here in the year 19… 14!
> Here in the year 19… 14! [*started by* MAUDE]
> Here in the year 19… 14! [*started by* ALLARKINI]

CHARLIE and BONES *start up their interlocutor/end man routine.*

BONES: What you waitin' on, Boss?
CHARLIE: Well, Bones, as usual I'm waiting on my wife. She sure is late for this picnic.
BONES: You knows womens, Boss.
CHARLIE: You're a smart old coon, Bones, why is it a man's wife has to be so different to his mother?
BONES: Well, a man's mother takes care of him, Boss. And a man's wife takes care of his wallet.
CHARLIE: Not my wife, Bones. She doesn't pay any attention to my wallet.
BONES: You is a lucky man, Boss.
CHARLIE: She's too busy taking care of Mr Smith's trousers, from next door.
BONES: It's good you found yourself a neighbourly woman.
CHARLIE: That's what the neighbours say.

Meanwhile, KNUCKLES *has begun to pile chairs on top of each other.* CHARLIE *sees where he is doing it and hisses at him under his breath:*

Knuckles—not there.

KNUCKLES *looks at him questioningly,* CHARLIE *continues to glare at him, indicating with his head to move the act further to the right.* KNUCKLES *doesn't get it. Furiously,* CHARLIE *indicates something about the floor, all the while, constantly turning and smiling at the audience.* KNUCKLES *finally gets it and begins to move.* CHARLIE *turns to the audience.*

Knuckles, what life-risking, devil-may-care great act of courage are you putting your neck on the line with for us this evening?

KNUCKLES *doesn't answer, but awkwardly presents the chairs.*

No! Not the Mountain of Moses! That's the most dangerous feat there is! I forbid you, Knuckles! I absolutely forbid you from attempting the Mountain of Moses here in this theatre.

KNUCKLES *looks at* CHARLIE *sadly. Nods his head, then hangs it down and begins to pack up the act.* CHARLIE *looks horrified, but tries to keep a smiling face for the audience. He speaks out of the corner of his mouth.*

What are you doing, Knuckles?

KNUCKLES *indicates that he is packing up.* CHARLIE *growls at him out of the corner of his mouth.*

Do that act, Knuckles.

KNUCKLES *nods, happily and begins to set up the act again.*

CHARLIE *watches him with mock horror and speaks loudly for the benefit of the audience.*

Knuckles! I told you that as your brother and the owner of this theatre I forbid you— Why, has anyone ever attempted Moses Mountain and lived? I think not. No, Knuckles, I cannot permit you to almost certainly perish upon this stage tonight, simply for the utter delight of our audience. You hear me—I forbid you to attempt the Mountain of Moses!

KNUCKLES *again looks sad. He nods, hangs his head and begins to pack up the act.*

CHARLIE *looks incredulous and furiously. He whispers out of the side of his mouth.*

Do the bleedin' act, Knuckles. Do it!

KNUCKLES *looks confused for a moment, then smiles. And sets the act up and begins.*

CHARLIE *speaks to the audience:*
Well, ladies and gentlemen, it looks as though there's no stopping him. Knuckles is determined to entertain you beyond your wildest dreams even if it means that he will ever likely snap apart and die right here in front of your eyes.

KNUCKLES *begins the chair balancing act. At the very beginning his foot goes through a floorboard. He looks at* CHARLIE *nervously.* CHARLIE *again speaks out of the corner of his mouth.*

ALLARKINI *looks very interested in this broken floorboard. He begins to inch closer.*

That's why I said over there. [*Turning back to the audience*] The more danger, the more compelled Knuckles is. He's very much alike to one of those big-winged insects that get drawn to fire—
BONES: Moth to the flame, Boss?
CHARLIE: Um, no. Not exactly. Close, but that's not exactly what I meant. I was thinking of a different kind of winged insect. I believe it was closer to a dragonfly. Though well done, Mr Bones.

KNUCKLES *is climbing higher and higher.* ALLARKINI, *ever since the floorboard breaking, has been inching closer and closer to the break. As* KNUCKLES *is high up on the chairs,* ALLARKINI *gets onto his knees and begins to lift the broken floorboard. He rolls up his sleeve, and begins to get ready to put his hand down there.*

He slowly reaches it in. He feels something. Something terrible. He stops, frozen still. CHARLIE *sees what he is doing.*

Great God! He's a madman! Allarkini—move away! Move away from the Mountain of Moses this instant!

ALLARKINI *is frozen there.* CHARLIE *rushes over and begins to pull him away.*

ALLARKINI: I feel it. I find it. I know vat I feel.
CHARLIE: You'll cause the mountain to topple, you half-baked wizard!

A scuffle is caused as CHARLIE *pulls* ALLARKINI *away—causing more floorboards to break.*

VIOLET *gasps. The chairs shake, but at the last moment,* KNUCKLES *lands safely in a chair.*

VIOLET, *despite herself, claps. They all stare at her.* ALLARKINI *laughs bitterly.*

He's survived! My dear brother has survived! Count yourselves lucky, folks, as I must tell you—I will never—never permit him to attempt such a feat again! And now for some light entertainment let's hear from Maude and her little dummy Doris.

DORIS: Hey! Who are you calling light entertainment—and come to think of it—who are you calling a dummy?

MAUDE *and* DORIS *go into their act.*

MAUDE: Doris, you came in very late last night. I demand to know where you were.

DORIS: Oh, don't worry, Maude, it weren't like I were out there alone.

MAUDE: That's precisely what I'm worried about! Don't tell me, Doris, you better not tell me you were in the slums of Collingwood last night. [*She waits.*] Well?!

DORIS: You said don't tell you.

MAUDE: You know how I feel about the Irish, Doris.

DORIS: But what you don't know is how the Irish feel deep inside me.

MAUDE: They like to take a drink from the bottle.

DORIS: I prefer to take the whole bottle meself.

MAUDE: Oh, Doris, whatever shall I do with you?

DORIS: Nothin' that ain't already been done to me last night—that's one thing for certain!

MAUDE: Well, what's done is done I suppose. So all we can do is our best to undo it. Let us make our way to the church.

DORIS: Alright, but may we make it a Catholic Church?

MAUDE: But we're not Catholic, Doris.

DORIS: Well, that gives us something to confess right off the bat!

MAUDE: I know why you want to be a Catholic, Doris—it's those Irish boys!

DORIS: You're wrong. It's the priests. I love a man in uniform.

MAUDE: Speaking of uniforms, have you noticed how smart that soldier looks in his uniform? Now there's a fine young man. Doing his part for his country.

DORIS: I'd like to have his part in my country.

MAUDE *grows more and more distressed by* DORIS*'s answers.*

MAUDE: What will you do for your part, Doris?
DORIS: I could be a nurse. I can tell that lots of those soldiers need relief.
MAUDE: Well, I suppose you could dress their open wounds.
DORIS: That's right! And I could let them undress mine. Get it? My open wound? I could get the private to undress my parts! Get it? Private part? They're the privates and I've got the parts and they've got private parts too—

CHARLIE *breaks in:*

CHARLIE: Speaking of songs—
BONES: Was we?
CHARLIE: What?
BONES: Was we speaking of songs, Boss?
CHARLIE: That's your cue, Bones.
BONES: I knows, Boss, but I did not hear you speaking directly of songs—so I was somewhat confused as to the nature of my next duty.
CHARLIE: Play the song, Mr Bones.
BONES: Well, that clears it up somewhat now, Mr Charlie. I'm sorry, but I's only gots the mind of a coon.
CHARLIE: And the big mouth of one too!

As MAUDE *and* DORIS *begin to sing the 'Pony' song,* ALLARKINI *and* KNUCKLES *come out as a sort of pantomime horse. They do a dance.* ALLARKINI'S *face is visible, and he does not look at all pleased.*

CHARLIE *keeps attempting to mount the horse, but* ALLARKINI *always moves at the last moment. This is making* CHARLIE *quite angry. However,* MAUDE *continues to look lovingly at* ALLARKINI *the horse throughout the song.*

MAUDE: I had a little pony, my pony's name was Tony
          And every day I'd ride him
DORIS: Every day she'd ride him
MAUDE: Bumping all the while, he'd always make me smile as
          Every day I'd ride him
DORIS: Every day she'd ride him
MAUDE: When I was a girl, he was my world
          He taught me everything there was to know

DORIS:	You can say that again
MAUDE:	Doris!
	He'd nuzzle up to me, oh-oh so kind
DORIS:	And take me roughly from behind
MAUDE:	Doris! That's not the words
ALL:	He'd take her from behind
MAUDE:	No, no, that's wrong!
	Now that Tony's gone, I know he'll linger on
	He'll always be inside me
DORIS:	He'll always be inside her!
MAUDE:	I always wear a smile
DORIS:	A secret sideways smile!
MAUDE:	He'll always be inside me
DORIS:	Always up inside her!
MAUDE:	Though the years have flown, and I have grown
	I always will remember
DORIS:	His massive horsey member
MAUDE:	Doris!
	There never was a friend so good and proud
DORIS:	And so mightily endowed
MAUDE:	Doris, what do you mean?
ALL:	The horse was well endowed
MAUDE:	I know one day I'll find a man
	Who's good and warm and kind
	And he will choose to walk beside me
DORIS:	And like a pony he will ride me
MAUDE:	And I will be the gladdest girl in all the world.	DORIS: Who I think she's on heat
MAUDE:	In all the world	DORIS: She gagging for it
MAUDE:	In all the world.	DORIS: Oh ya filthy slut!

MAUDE *is desperately trying to stop* DORIS, *trying to cover her mouth, but* DORIS *won't be stopped.* CHARLIE *has to try and help her. He signals* VIOLET *to help too.* DORIS *bites* VIOLET *on the hand.*

VIOLET *is shocked, she cannot pull her hand away from* DORIS. DORIS *is muttering garbled obscenities.*

CHARLIE: Ha ha! What a finale to the song! [*Out of the corner of his mouth*] Let go now, Doris.

> DORIS *does not let go.* CHARLIE *speaks to* BONES *and the audience, in between trying to casually pry* DORIS *off of* VIOLET*'s hand.*

Bones, you know who I saw just the other day?

BONES: Who's that, Boss?

CHARLIE: I saw Mr Cohen standing out on the street yesterday with a large case. I asked him what was inside it. He told me it was full of old photograph albums, the only thing he'd saved when his house burnt down. He looked a little shaken, which was unusual for him after a fire. When I asked him what the matter was, he told me he'd had a tough time making the decision on choosing to rescue his photograph album rather than other items of importance from the burning house. He asked me if I thought he'd saved the right thing. I told him he had, seeing as memories are the only thing his 500 pounds insurance money won't buy back. He looked relieved and cried out, 'You see! I told my wife we could get another daughter!'

> ALLARKINI *has been struggling to get out of the horse suit for some time. Finally he is out.*
>
> DORIS *begrudgingly lets go of* VIOLET*'s hand.* VIOLET *stands, holding her hand.*

ALLARKINI: Ha ha! Funny.

> *He speaks to* DORIS. DORIS *begrudgingly lets go.* VIOLET *stands, holding her hand.*

I have joke. I have joke about one theatre owner.

CHARLIE: You don't say.

ALLARKINI: Charlie Mudd.

CHARLIE: Yes?

ALLARKINI: This is the joke.

CHARLIE: I see. Well, that's very funny.

ALLARKINI: I am not the comedian. I am the magician,

CHARLIE: Yes.

ALLARKINI: But I make the joke.

CHARLIE: It was very funny, Allarkini.

ALLARKINI: The punch line of this joke is Charlie Mudd and his theatre.
CHARLIE: I have a joke too, Allarkini. Would you like to hear it?
ALLARKINI: Please indulge me, Mr Mudd.
CHARLIE: The great magician Allarkini.
ALLARKINI: Yes?
CHARLIE: That is the joke.
ALLARKINI: I am the great magician Allarkini!
CHARLIE: And that is the joke.

> ALLARKINI *furiously bursts into song. As* ALLARKINI *sings,* CHARLIE *rushes behind a prop or set piece. Meanwhile* MAUDE *and* KNUCKLES *help* VIOLET *to change clothes so that she is dressed like a man.*

ALLARKINI: Countess Elizabeth Bathory hung 600 virgins on hooks // [*clap clap*]
From her ceiling [*baa-dum, bum bum baa-dum*]
Some of these girls were peasants taken from their homes in the middle of the night // [*clap clap*]
Some were noble [*baa-dum, bum bum bum*]
She drained their blood for to drink and bathe
And disposed of their bodies in nefarious ways
She was never ever sorry, even when she was caught [*pause*]
And locked in a cupboard four years [*clap clap*]
Where she died [*clap clap*]
All alone [*clap clap*]
Unrepentant
It's said there's never been [*pause*] in all history
Never been anyone more evil,
Than the countess of Bathory
But I know o-o-o-o-ne
His name is Charlie Mudd! [*bum baa-dum, bum bum baa-dum*]

Attila the Hun killed a lot of men then he raped their wives
And their daughters // [*clap*] and their horses
He'd go into battle and corner his man and tear out his eyes
And his liver // [*clap*] and he'd eat it
He even killed his brother who shared his throne
Had him shot in a forest where he died all alone

He was never ever sorry, he was always right
He thought the world was his [*clap clap*]
And he was killed [*clap clap*]
By his wife [*clap clap*]
She stabbed him [*scream*]
Who could blame her?
It is said there's never been [*pause*] in all history
Never been a man more ruthless
Than Attila Attila the Hun
But I know o-o-o-one
His name is Charlie Mudd! [bum baa-dum, bum bum baa-dum]

What Cain did to Abel
What the snake did to Eve
What the Jews did to Jesus
What the plague did to Europe
Like the richer to the poorer
Jack the Ripper to the whore-a
Like the boss to his worker
Dr Crippen to his Cora
All these things are very bad
Yes they're very very bad
But not so bad
Not nearly so bad
No nothing's so bad
As my good friend
My very good friend
My good friend, good friend
My very good friend
My good friend Charlie Mudd!

ALLARKINI *finishes the song.*

CHARLIE *quickly speaks, from behind the set piece.*

CHARLIE: That was the Great Allarkini with the famous Russian ballad sung in honour of old friends. And now, ladies and gentlemen, be prepared to be utterly mystified as this same Great Allarkini unleashes his powers, right here, before our very eyes. [*Whispering to* ALLARKINI] And keep it nice.

ALLARKINI: I, the Great Allarkini who have travelled many a sea. Yes, the Great Allarkini has known the likes of Harry Houdini. But I tell you—Harry Houdini—is man of science! Not man of magic. I, the Great Allarkini am man of magic. But yes, it is plague onto me. For live only I can in the places where magic may to survive. These place, they are to last, one, two minute in time. And then, gone. This magic I show you… is so horrible… so horrible that one time an old lady who watch it—she die. And one day a little boy who watch it, he try to copy. And he die. It is this magic that will one day—perhaps today—end the life of the Great Allarkini. We begin.

KNUCKLES, acting as the assistant, rolls up one of ALLARKINI*'s sleeves.*

He hands him a small razor. ALLARKINI *makes an incision on his inner forearm.*

KNUCKLES *hands him a straw. He sticks the straw into the incision. He begins to suck at it, spitting out blood as he does so. This goes on for some time.*

He looks up at where the audience sit.

Some time take longer than others.

He begins again. Sucking, spitting blood. Finally comes up for air.

I will need wider straw.

KNUCKLES *presents him with a wider straw.*

He sucks and sucks again.

Finally, he pulls out, through the straw, a very long worm.

KNUCKLES *assists him, with a handkerchief.*

They keep pulling and pulling the worm. It is obscenely long. ALLARKINI *and* KNUCKLES *present it, as they would a rabbit that's turned into a dove.*

As ALLARKINI *presents the worm towards the audience,* MAUDE *cries out, like a teenage fan:*

MAUDE: The Great Allarkini!

The others all stare at her.

ALLARKINI: All these parasites ladies and gentlemen, are alive in this theatre. But it should not be that they are here. Must be that something very wrong that these parasite be here…
CHARLIE: Thank you, Allarkini, for stunning us all with your worms—
ALLARKINI: But I'm not finished.
CHARLIE: You'll be more than finished in a minute. And now the act you've all been waiting for. It's an exciting time in the evening, ladies and gentlemen. It is with great pleasure that I present the dramatic duologue, 'The Sitting Lady and the Picnicking Gent', starring everyone's darling, Ethelyn Rarity.

> VIOLET *has a script. She is dressed as a man.* CHARLIE *is dressed as a woman. He moves very delicately and looks quite demure.*
>
> CHARLIE *speaks in a sweet, female voice.* VIOLET *speaks in a deep, masculine voice.* CHARLIE *stands by the picture of the river, looking demure. Everyone else watches, fixatedly, but from further away on the stage.*
>
> VIOLET, *the man, approaches* CHARLIE, *the woman.*

VIOLET: Hello, my lady. May I enquire what you are doing?
CHARLIE: Can't you see? I'm passing the time by the river. What more ought a lady to be doing?
VIOLET: Yet, why are you on your lonesome?
CHARLIE: What company do I have worth keeping? What company would I rather than my own and Swanston River.
VIOLET: One could argue that neither you nor the river are company to yourself.
CHARLIE: I take offence on that, good sir.
VIOLET: Don't. It's just I worry you may fall prey to obnoxious types, sitting here all on your own.

> VIOLET *sits beside him.*

CHARLIE: None came along until you.
VIOLET: And now that I'm here, I shall see that they don't.
CHARLIE: How very kind of you, but it's time that I were going.
VIOLET: Going where?
CHARLIE: I have a ticket aboard the *SS Tivoli*.
VIOLET: The *SS Tivoli*?

CHARLIE: The famous showboat. Haven't you heard, it's sailing by here, on its way to all other places of the world. And I'm going to catch it.
VIOLET: How long until the *SS Tivoli* passes here again?
CHARLIE: Not until forever, I suppose.
VIOLET: I shall miss you. First, will you share my picnic lunch with me?
CHARLIE: But, my good man, it is far past lunchtime.
VIOLET: The lunch won't know. Don't tell the chicken! Really, have some chicken, won't you?
CHARLIE: I'm frightened.
VIOLET: It's cooked all the way through. And there are no remaining feathers stuck in it.
CHARLIE: It's not your chicken that frightens me.
VIOLET: Is it I? Am I frightening to you, little dove?
CHARLIE: No. I'm not frightened of you. But I'm frightened to stay too long… I don't want to miss the boat. And I've heard of some terrible things happening here by the river after dark.
VIOLET: Have you been to the old theatre?
CHARLIE: The old theatre?
VIOLET: It's apparently very beautiful. On the outside, it's made up to look like a castle. Imagine that! A castle! On the river.
CHARLIE: I didn't know there was a theatre on this river.
VIOLET: Walk down the riverbed with me. And by and by, we'll come to it.
CHARLIE: I must catch the ship…
VIOLET: Yes. But first, you'll come with me. What's your name, little dove—let me guess, it's… [*She becomes a woman again. She speaks to herself.*] Ethelyn. My name is Ethelyn.

The artistes look at her, understanding. They begin to sing a song.

ARTISTES: Here's another one, have another one, here's another one now.
    Oh, here's another one, have another one, here's another one now.
    Oh, here's another one, have another one, here's another one now.

By the end of the song, VIOLET *is very different. There is something sexier, but more broken about her.*

CHARLIE *and* VIOLET *stare into each other.* CHARLIE *steps towards her.*

CHARLIE: Ethelyn…
VIOLET: Charlie…

> *He pushes her back against a wall, as though about to kiss her. They pause like that for one moment. Their faces right up close to each other.* VIOLET *'wakes up'. She jolts.*

I don't—I don't know my lines.
CHARLIE: You don't have to say anything, Ethelyn.
VIOLET: I have to go. I don't know my lines—
CHARLIE: But all you need to do is stand still. Very still.

> *He moves away from her.*

DORIS: Stand still, Ethelyn. Very still.

> *Knives begin to be thrown at her.* KNUCKLES *is throwing knives at her.*

CHARLIE: Is there anything this wonder of a man cannot do, ladies and gentlemen? Observe—the precise—the cunning of his toss. And look, at the fear in her eye. Surely, just the tip of one of these razor-sharp knives would be enough to rip her in two.

> VIOLET *looks terrified. She calls out:*

VIOLET: I—I don't know my lines here…
MAUDE: Just stay still, Ethelyn. Very, very still. And he's sure to miss you every time.
ALLARKINI: Cruelty. Such cruelty to the Ethelyn. Poor things. She is no smarter than animal. Stay still, poor Ethelyn. Stay very still.

> *The knife throwing ends.* VIOLET *is surrounded by knives sticking out all around her frame.*
>
> *She is shaking.* CHARLIE *says an aside to her:*

CHARLIE: You were wonderful.
ALLARKINI: Tonight, for special treat, the Great Allarkini presents second magic—
CHARLIE: Ladies and gentlemen, it is now time for interval—
ALLARKINI: There is something which have grown rotten in this theatre. It is on the breath of my fellow artistes.

> *He presents the long worm again.*

CHARLIE: They've seen your worm already, Allarkini.

ALLARKINI: My friend worm his way to bottom of these secret. But worm have not the words to tell the Great Allarkini what are these secret that he see. Mr Charlie Mudd, The Great Allarkini look now for secret—in your mind.

CHARLIE: Ha ha, he's joking of course.

>KNUCKLES *looks up at* ALLARKINI, *hurt and angry.*

ALLARKINI: Come, what are you frightened of, Mr Interlocutor? It must be a very wicked secret, yes? If you cannot share it with the artistes you share your theatre with. Whose hard work creates your very livelihood! If you are a man of honour, the truth hold no fear for you, Charlie Mudd.

>*He introduces his magic contraption. It is revealed or brought out.*

Mr Charlie Mudd, you must to step up now to my Machine of Unhappy. It want to look upon your soul and see the secret there. This Machine of Unhappy it find the ghost that haunt of all man mind and bring it dance onto his face and limb. The magic of the never was and was once, but was not once again.

CHARLIE: It is a secret, Allarkini, that you do not really wish to see.

>ALLARKINI *is in a way, hypnotising* CHARLIE.

ALLARKINI: Mr Charlie Mudd, you must to step up now to my machine.

CHARLIE: It is a secret, Allarkini, that might kill you if you see.

ALLARKINI: Mr Charlie Mudd, you must to step up now to my machine.

>CHARLIE, *in a hypnotised-like state, begins to step into the Machine of Unhappy.*

>KNUCKLES *growls at* ALLARKINI—*coiled to attack.*

CHARLIE: It's alright, Knuckles. I will step up onto the Great Allarkini's machine. But let it be known and said whose shoulders will have to wear this—and it will hang on his head.

>*He sits in the machine.* ALLARKINI, *with* MAUDE *and* DORIS*'s assistance, fasten him in.* ALLARKINI *begins a spell.*

You think I robbed you what should have been yours.
But without me, Allarkini, your dreams are just dust.
A dust on the props, a dust on the floor.

A dust that blew away if one opened the door.
You talk of honour and things a man should have done.
But without me, Allarkini, you'd have no battle lost, no battle won.
You'd be a soldier searching the lands for a war,
An empty rifle, a ship moored on the shore.

ALLARKINI: Mr Charlie Mudd, who has stepped up now to my machine. Will show us others these very things you dream.

> ALLARKINI *conjures. The whole of Mudd's Castle fills with magic— perhaps it even shakes a little.*
>
> CHARLIE *is being drawn deep into something. He begins to shake. To convulse, as though he were possessed. His face changes.*
>
> CHARLIE *begins to speak in several different voices. In the beginning he is speaking only as himself and* ETHELYN, *but then other voices come into it too.*

CHARLIE: Eight o'clock... everything begins... at eight o'clock... Ethelyn ... you look beautiful. You're still my star... aren't you, darling?
[*As* ETHELYN] No-one who's safe is ever happy. And no-one who's happy is safe.
[*As* MAUDE] Each lonely footstep that came up on the stair...
[*As* DORIS] But you must get lonely, out there on the stage, all alone?
[*As* ALLARKINI] The food... the food of the worm...
[*In a ghostly voice*] I've been waiting in all the darkest places at night. I've been waiting for the lights to come back.
[*As* BONES] It ain't right, Miss Ethelyn, a coon like me
[*In a ghostly voice*] My feet are wet. My feet are always wet. I changed my stockings. I change my slippers. I change my wooden shoes. But they are always wet. This stage is so, so damp.
[*As* ETHELYN] Who are you? Who are you to refuse me? All the men in this theatre are ridiculous.
[*As* MAUDE] Are you sure she won't mind, Doris?
[*As* ETHELYN] She should be in the lunatic asylum.
[*As* DORIS] And you calls yourself a man of honour! Treachery! Treachery!
[*As* CHARLIE] You can't really be thinking of leaving, can you, my dear? You must have known I'd never let you go. You see, look around you. No-one is leaving. No-one.

He makes the sound of several different screams.
[*As* ETHELYN] I could have been a star.
[*As* CHARLIE] I made everything into nothing so that I could be something.
So you should be here too. Just one more show… Bring me my gun. Don't touch that door. Don't you dare touch that door. If you… if you open that door…
[*As* ALLARKINI] It is a secret, that kill me to see.

And then CHARLIE *begins to choke, as though on smoke. His eyes bulge in his head. As his body hacks and coughs.*

VIOLET *looks at them all. They are all watching, in poses.*

VIOLET: Won't someone help him?

They stare blankly back at her.

Mister Bones?

BONES *looks down at his piano.* VIOLET *walks slowly up to* CHARLIE. *She puts her hand on him.*

Mr Mudd? Mr Mudd? I'm frightfully worried for you… Something dreadful is happening… Mr Mudd…

She shakes him. He looks up at her once. He reaches up and touches her face.

CHARLIE: Ethelyn?
VIOLET: Mr Mudd…
CHARLIE: Just one more show…

VIOLET *looks afraid.*

VIOLET: Well, someone help him!

KNUCKLES *rushes over, and lies his head in* CHARLIE*'s lap, like a dog.* VIOLET *looks out into the audience, as though looking for help.*

She calls out into the audience:

Help him—is there a doctor in the house—won't you help him…

Another kind of expression comes over her face. And she walks slowly towards the footlights. She is squinting. As though she is looking into the sun. She walks closer and closer to the footlights. She stands at the edge of them, looking out into the audience.

There's... there's no-one out there.
MAUDE: You're wrong, my dear. They're out there. Watching us.
VIOLET: No. It's empty. [*She looks afraid.*] Why can't you see—you must see—there's no-one out there.
MAUDE: There are eyes in the dark that never close. Just as one may never turn off the stars that shine at night.
DORIS: They're still here. Applauding us. Can't you hear them? That cheeky devil in the stalls is looking right up my skirt! Take me a little closer will ya, Maude—he seems to be near-sighted.

KNUCKLES *does a slow and eerie trick.*

BONES: The magic of the minstrel show will never die. So long as we feed it with our own blood—feed it with our lives—it never die.
VIOLET: I have to go. I have to go now.
ALLARKINI: No, my dear. You cannot go. We must find out.

A dress appears. The dress a star would wear. It floats down to VIOLET. *It is Ethelyn's dress. It collapses, into* VIOLET's *arms.*

DORIS: Put on your costume, Ethelyn.

ALLARKINI *and* MAUDE *are closing in on her.* KNUCKLES, *who was sobbing into* CHARLIE's *lap, gets up and begins to round in on her too.* BONES *keeps playing his piano.*

VIOLET *runs to the forbidden door, but before she gets there,* KNUCKLES *is in front of it, snarling.*

She suddenly gets an idea and runs towards the front of the stage.

But before she gets there, she is surrounded.

They begin to close in on her.

BONES: You has to stay, Miss Ethelyn. We needs you. We needs you to do the show.

They slowly close the curtain. CHARLIE *lies, semi-conscious, muttering.*

END OF ACT ONE

ACT TWO

SCENE ONE

For a moment the stage in front of the closed red curtain is empty. And in that emptiness there is the loud sound of a clap of thunder. And then the sound of heavy rain. There is no need for the sound of the rain to be continuous, it should just come in every now and then as a reminder.

The red curtain remains closed. Now CHARLIE *is alone in front of the red curtain. He is mopping up water. He is wearing a raincoat. He has a bucket and a mop.*

CHARLIE: Say, Bones?
BONES: Yes, Boss?
CHARLIE: Do you remember the first night of Mudd's Castle?
BONES: Yes, Boss.
CHARLIE: There was a line of people from the front door to halfway down Swanston River. And it was a perfect night too. You remember, Bones, the stars were bright and the sky was clear and the air was sharp too.
BONES: I remember, Boss.
CHARLIE: And what a show we put on for them, huh Bones?

> *He sings a song.*
>
> Why should I now be alone?
> Haven't I built everything, to make this place a home
> I've given up my life, I've given everything I own, so I say
> Why should I now be alone?
>
> *He speaks to* BONES.

Do you remember, Bones, it was the fifth time we'd come out to bow—they wouldn't let us go. We were hollering out to them—'Go home—we've gotta get our beauty sleep too!' And they'd just howl back laughin' and stomp their feet—all of them standing—all of them—and that one little lady—you remember her—you must remember her, Bones—she was in the second row—wearing that hat that was too big for her head—that hat with the red rose in it—

well, you remember—she plucked that rose right outa her hat and threw it into the air. Where it spun around three times—and where did it land—I caught it right in my mouth! Well, after that no-one was going home without another song.

He sings again.

> I've sung my heart out to the public's ears
> I've stretched my throat in hope I'd wring out some tears
> I've packed up all my youngest years
> And sent them on their way
> And so I say…

BONES: What do you say, Boss?

CHARLIE: Why should I now be alone?

CHARLIE: [*singing*] Though the curtains now are faded and the orchestra's gone home

BONES: Because you didn't pay 'em, Boss.

CHARLIE [*singing*] But who needs an orchestra when you've a coon like Bones.

BONES: You didn't pay me for a while now either.

CHARLIE: [*spoken*] That's enough now,
   [*Sung*] What I'm trying to say is
   Why should I now be alone?

He speaks, lighting up as he remembers the good times.

And I thought to myself that night, well this is it. This is what it feels like to be standing here in your dream, as it comes true right beneath your feet. And that was how it was always gonna be. Oh, I was sure of that.

He sings again.

> And so I say
> Why should I now be alone?
> Though the crowds are thinning and my theatre's not well-known
> With just a little faith, this place will stand up on its own
> Why should I now be alone?
> Why should I now be alone?

CHARLIE *finishes the song.*

SCENE TWO

CHARLIE *speaks as though to an audience.*

CHARLIE: Why must nature prey on all things gentle? Why must innocence be punished so severely? Time and time again we have learnt from this world of ours that the kind must suffer at the hands of the hungry. But so many hands, ladies and gentlemen? Must there be so many hands…

The red curtain opens.

… so many hands on the huntsman?

Once the curtain is opened, there is ETHELYN. *She dances in an oblivious, pretty way, as a butterfly.*

The piano music changes, and a creeping comes into it. KNUCKLES, *as a giant spider, begins to stalk her. Perhaps he creeps down the wall as she dances, oblivious, across the stage.*

He will creep up on her, or dangle down to her, almost seize her, when just in the nick of time she'll flap elsewhere to sniff a flower.

This continues for some time, growing darker and more ominous.

At last, KNUCKLES *the spider finally catches* ETHELYN *the butterfly. He begins to kill her, in a dance-like way, strangling her.*

Slowly, petitely, she is dying.

The butterfly dies. She lies there for a moment. And then, in a split second, ETHELYN'S *eyes open and she has grabbed* KNUCKLES *around the throat.*

ETHELYN: Too hard!

In moments, she is on top of him, strangling him.

How do you like it when I squeeze your windpipe, halfwit? Every time I tell you and you never learn. Maybe this time you'll remember not to squeeze too hard!

KNUCKLES *is struggling beneath* ETHELYN. *She starts to kick him. A voice from the darkness—behind the backcloth.*

DORIS: You're not his mummy, Ethelyn. You're as barren as the wind.

ETHELYN *stands up, furious. She storms over to the backcloth and yanks it down. When the backcloth comes down, it reveals the workings of the theatre behind—Charlie's office, dressing tables, Allarkini's nook with his magic contraptions.*

ALLARKINI *is leaning over one of his machines, in his undergarments, dismayed, trying to make it work. He hasn't seemed to notice any of the commotion, because he is so entrenched in making something work.* MAUDE *and* DORIS *are in Ethelyn's dressing-room, looking through her things.*

ETHELYN: In my dressing-room, no less. [*To* DORIS] You perverted piece of pine.

DORIS: Just using your comb.

MAUDE: You have such lovely hair, Ethelyn.

DORIS: Yeah, because it hides her face.

ETHELYN: Now listen here, you over-celebrated piece of firewood—

Just then, ALLARKINI *gets his contraption to work. And he appears beside them all, in a puff of smoke.*

ALLARKINI: Here I have appeared. From the burning coals of Alaska to save one poor, innocent butterfly.

They all stare at ALLARKINI. *He surveys the scene.* ETHELYN *shrugs and begins to kick* KNUCKLES *again.*

I am supposed to save butterfly. Not spider.

ETHELYN: We've made some changes. Get used to it.

She continues to kick KNUCKLES.

ALLARKINI: I have taken so much of my magic to appear like so and now the act has changed. Charlie Mudd—how can the Great Allarkini work under such amateur condition? Mudd!

CHARLIE *enters.*

ETHELYN: He choked me again. He does it on purpose, Charlie.

CHARLIE: On purpose? You're mad. Besides, if the Great Allarkini had appeared when he was supposed to appear, this little alteration to the act would not be happening.

ALLARKINI: The magic come when the magic come.

CHARLIE: Funny, I never heard of Harry Houdini having any trouble controlling his magic.

ALLARKINI: No—because his magic is the fake! You want the real magic—it is unpredict!

CHARLIE: I don't want the real magic. I want what's going to make the audience happy tonight.

ALLARKINI: You ask the Great Allarkini to perform the fake magic.

CHARLIE: Tonight we do whatever it takes to make the show a hit. Do you understand?

He finally gets ETHELYN *off* KNUCKLES.

ALLARKINI: Why should I to listen to you, Mister Mudd? You, the killer of dreams.

CHARLIE: Because tonight is a special night.

ETHELYN *stops fighting for a moment. She looks at* CHARLIE, *touched.*

ETHELYN: [*tenderly*] Charlie, you remembered.

CHARLIE: Of course I remembered.

She touches his face.

I've been killing myself working on this for weeks. But I've just got confirmation—I've got him.

ETHELYN: Him? Who's him?

CHARLIE: Golden Touch Robbins.

ALLARKINI: Not Golden Touch Robbins who promote the final show of the Great Lafayette—the final show before he die in the legend of fire…

BONES: Not Golden Touch Robbins who teach the famous Mr Tambo how to dance?

MAUDE: Not Golden Touch Robbins who toured that whole circus of broken-hearted orphans until every single of one them had a home?

CHARLIE: That's him.

ALLARKINI: You are crazy, Mudd.

CHARLIE *holds out a telegram.* ALLARKINI *grabs it from him. He reads it.*

He looks up before reading out loud.

Dear Mister Mudd, I accept your invitation to visit Mudd's Castle. I have been aware of your theatre for some time and would be very interested to see if there might be a way we could come to an agreement which would be beneficial to all involved.

He looks up.

It is true. His signature. In the gold. Not one can copy this signature. Not even the magic. It say here—he come tonight.

CHARLIE: If we make it work tonight—if we make the show sparkle—remember—like it used to sparkle—then we'll be back. Back in business. So tonight, Allarkini, pull a damn rabbit out of your hat.

MAUDE: Mr Mudd... what does he look like—this Golden Touch Robbins—

DORIS: I could do a special show just for him, if ya get what I mean...

CHARLIE: All I know... is he wears a golden coat...

BONES: Do you really think he'll like the show?

CHARLIE: Are you kidding? He'll love it. He'll take care of things with the river. He'll clean up the mud. He'll stop the flooding. My word, this man can probably even stop the rain.

DORIS *laughs.*

And then the audiences will flock back. They'll hear how tremendous you all are. The seats will be filled. Your pay will be doubled—

ALLARKINI: Ha, double of nothing.

CHARLIE: My word.

ETHELYN *laughs. She laughs until they all look at her. And then she stops.*

Did I say something amusing, Ethelyn?

ETHELYN: Hugh D. Macintosh begged me to be the star of his theatre. To perform amongst the best vaudeville acts of the world. And I came [*bursting into laughter again*] here. I'm not laughing at you, Charlie. I'm laughing at myself. I could have been performing to hundreds—hundreds of people tonight. Instead I'm here with a bunch of no-hopers and an audience full to the brim of empty seats.

DORIS: If Hugh D. Macintosh wants you so much why don't you just go there now and give our ears a rest!

CHARLIE: Ethelyn—this time we are on the brink of success. Golden Touch Robbins can make us more popular than any theatre of Hugh D. Macintosh's. Everyone will know about Mudd's Castle.

ETHELYN: No. Charlie. They won't.

CHARLIE: They won't?

ETHELYN: No-one will remember Mudd's Castle. Tonight will be like every other night. [*She begins to walk out.*] Except that it's our anniversary.

CHARLIE: Our anniversary... Ethelyn!

> ETHELYN *leaves.*
>
> KNUCKLES *looks around, ends up going underneath the stage.*
> CHARLIE *doesn't see him go down.*

Now, get your acts right—to where they could be—just imagine all those eyes—delighting—all those eyes! Everything counts on it. Everything. We have until eight p.m.

> *They all synchronise their ankle watches.*
>
> *They all scatter, to work on their acts. Except for* CHARLIE, *who remains.*
>
> *There is a loud crack of thunder.*

Knuckles—go and find her a present, would you?

> KNUCKLES *gestures: 'Like what?'*

I don't know... something pretty!

SCENE THREE

Everyone is getting ready in their dressing-rooms.

With the loud crack of thunder, KNUCKLES *emerges from beneath the stage, carrying a bunch of soaked and muddy flowers. He is also carrying a mud-smeared mirror. There is something peculiar about him. He looks very distraught. Shaken.*

CHARLIE *sees how strange and frightened* KNUCKLES *looks.* KNUCKLES *is covered in mud.*

KNUCKLES *shakes his head and looks away.*

CHARLIE: You're wet, Knuckles. Where have you been? That mirror—What else? What else did you see down there, Knuckles?

> KNUCKLES *doesn't look at* CHARLIE.

What else?

> KNUCKLES *looks down, and then suddenly, dry wretches, with his hand on his heart.*

> CHARLIE *rushes down, beneath the stage. He is gone only a few moments. He comes back up again, looking stricken. He walks to* KNUCKLES, *his hands dripping mud.*

> *He stands in front of* KNUCKLES *and grabs him on both arms—and looks him in the face.*

You saw. Didn't you, Knuckles?

> KNUCKLES *won't look at him.*

> KNUCKLES *nods his head. But he can't look at* CHARLIE.

> *A sudden sound of torrential rain.*

It's going to keep rising. The river's coming up through the theatre.

> KNUCKLES *dry wretches again. He tries to move away, but* CHARLIE *won't let him go.*

Knuckles. Stand up. I need your help. Do you understand me?

> KNUCKLES *shakes his head, not looking at* CHARLIE.

Do you think it's been easy? Bringing up a simple mute like you? You think the world wanted you, Knuckles? Your own parents deserted you. My parents. I lost my parents because of you, Knuckles. You have a responsibility to help me. To help your brother. Do you understand?

> KNUCKLES *nods.*

Do you understand?

> KNUCKLES *nods again. This time, he looks at* CHARLIE. *And then he hugs him. In a bear hug. And shivers against him.* CHARLIE *withstands it for a little while. And then pries away from him.*

> KNUCKLES *nods, proud now. He has pulled himself together.*

> CHARLIE *points to the mirror.*

Hide that. Don't move, brother.

> CHARLIE *hands* KNUCKLES *the muddy flowers and quickly disappears beneath the stage.*

SCENE FOUR

KNUCKLES *isn't sure what to do with the mirror. Shaken, he begins to look for places to hang it.*

And then he stops and looks into it. He has a moment with the mirror. Perhaps he does a handstand over it and lowers himself down to stare right into it. But his reflection doesn't comfort him, and he looks sadly up, while hovering above it.

SCENE FIVE

KNUCKLES *has become so distracted with the mirror that he doesn't hear or see* ETHELYN *approach. She and* KNUCKLES *both see each other at the same time.*

ETHELYN: You…

But before she can begin to berate KNUCKLES *she catches sight of herself in the mirror. She is mesmerised.*

What is this?

KNUCKLES *shakes his head, very nervous.*

ETHELYN, *transfixed by her reflection, takes the mirror from him. He hands it over to her. He goes to stomp his foot to warn* CHARLIE. *But* ETHELYN *says:*

Scram.

KNUCKLES *runs off in fear, guiltily looking back once over his shoulder and then disappearing.*

ETHELYN *looks into the mirror.*

And then, appearing in the mirror—a LONG AGO ETHELYN *looks back out at her. It is her, but different.*

ETHELYN *reaches her hand up to her face.* ETHELYN *falls into a sort of trance. She begins to sing.*

> Of all the other Ethelyns
> She's the prettiest one
> Of all the other Ethelyns
> She's the loveliest one
> Of all the other Ethelyns

Who've worn these borrowed clothes
Who've been and gone and sung this song
She is the fairest one
Of all the other Ethelyns
She is the loveliest one.

ETHELYN *places the mirror against the wall. The song stops.* LONG AGO ETHELYN, *in the mirror, speaks to her. She holds up a cigarette to her mouth in the mirror.*

LONG AGO ETHELYN: Do you have a light, darling?

ETHELYN *takes a match out of her pocket. She lights it and holds it to the mirror.*

Thank you.

LONG AGO ETHELYN *lights it. She begins to smoke.*

I became so addicted to these. You should try it. It's nice to have a focus outside of yourself.

ETHELYN: I have a focus outside of myself already.

LONG AGO ETHELYN: Ha ha. That's right. You're going to be a star. You came here. Here! Ha. Of all the places you came here to be a star.

ETHELYN: That's not what I meant.

LONG AGO ETHELYN: Oh. You love him, do you?

ETHELYN: I… I…

LONG AGO ETHELYN: They always fall for him. All you other Ethelyns. It's pitiful really. But I can help you. You see, I have something for you.

ETHELYN: You do?

LONG AGO ETHELYN: Tonight, the *SS Tivoli* will sail down Swanston River. You must have heard of the *SS Tivoli*?

ETHELYN: If you get a ticket on board the *SS Tivoli*—you're bound to be a star. If your act is on that deck you're guaranteed a place in every theatre in the world.

LONG AGO ETHELYN: At eight o'clock, it will sail to the door of Mudd's Castle to pick you up.

ETHELYN: Me? But why me?

LONG AGO ETHELYN: Don't you deserve to be a star?

ETHELYN: Yes… but eight o'clock is showtime. Charlie…

LONG AGO ETHELYN: Forget Charlie. How many times have you believed Charlie's empty promises? Do not wait for Golden Touch Robbins. Here is your ticket.

> LONG AGO ETHELYN *holds out a ticket to* ETHELYN *through the mirror.* ETHELYN *takes it.*
>
> LONG AGO ETHELYN *becomes* ETHELYN*'s reflection.*
>
> ETHELYN *holds the ticket out in front of her. She snaps out of her trance. She sees the ticket in her hand.*
>
> ALLARKINI *is absorbed in his magic box. Meanwhile, he doesn't see* ETHELYN, *who is staring into the mirror, in a trance.*
>
> ALLARKINI *is talking to himself.*
>
> *He stands with his arms outstretched—waiting for the magic to enter him. His eyes closed. He is more desperate in his voice this time.*

ALLARKINI: Magic, magic, come again. Come again to me. Oh, magic, magic, where are you? Come again to me? To your faithful and humbly servant, Allarkini. Magic, magic… please come back to me…

> *Nothing happens. He slouches over, defeated and heartsick.*
>
> *It is then, completely unaware of his presence, that* ETHELYN *looks back to the mirror where* LONG AGO ETHELYN *has reappeared.* LONG AGO ETHELYN *sings softly to her:*

LONG AGO ETHELYN:
>> Of all the other Ethelyns
>> Who've tarried on this stage
>> Their memories fade in this parade
>> As she commands this final page
>> Of all the other Ethelyns
>> She is the loveliest one
>> And of all the other Ethelyns
>> She is the loneliest one.

> ALLARKINI, *not knowing what it is, but feeling it or hearing it, has followed the song into* ETHELYN*'s dressing-room. He recognises the sound or feel of magic coming from her and the mirror.*

ALLARKINI: What did you say?

ETHELYN *snaps out of her trance. She looks over at* ALLARKINI. Just then. What is it you say?

ETHELYN: I didn't say a thing.

ALLARKINI approaches her.

ALLARKINI: Allarkini know. Allarkini know what is the sound of magic. Don't lie me.

He advances on her.

ETHELYN: Listen to me, you stale old wizard. I didn't say a thing.

Just then CHARLIE *reappears from beneath the stage. He is covered in mud. He looks stricken. He is dragging a huge, muddy sack. He sees* ALLARKINI *and* ETHELYN. *They don't see him.*

He is momentarily flabbergasted. He looks around for KNUCKLES *who is nowhere to be seen. He quickly pushes the sack back beneath the stage. And watches in secret.*

ALLARKINI *speaks softly to* ETHELYN. *His voice and words seem to be sort of hypnotising her. He steps right up close to her as he speaks.*

ALLARKINI: With enchanted eye, the Great Allarkini see in your heart terrible regret for wasted love. The Great Allarkini see in your brain great jumping of anger for wasted thought. With enchanted eye, the Great Allarkini see in your ear…

He reaches up slowly and tenderly pulls a long worm from her ear. The way a magician would pull a handkerchief from someone's ear. He holds it out, transfixed by it.

From inside her… It must to be… magic… Oh, thank you. Thank you for coming back to me. But why… why, magic, why… this long worm from inside her? [*He holds the worm out in front of him.*] But nevertheless. It is magic. Back to me.

But as he pulls the worm closer, a strange feeling comes over him, and he dry wretches, at the same time as holding onto his heart—as though it is broken and with his hand he is trying to repair it.

ETHELYN *stares at the worm, disgusted, but then suddenly a stronger feeling takes her over. She involuntarily dry wretches—*

she puts her hand to her heart as she does so—as though with her hand she is trying to stop a sad, beating feeling.

KNUCKLES *sneaks in and stands with* CHARLIE, *watching this whole interaction.*

ETHELYN: How dare you? How dare you put that sick thing by my face?

Shaking, she slaps ALLARKINI *on the cheek, hard.* MAUDE *and* DORIS *enter, seeing the slap.*

ALLARKINI *quickly conceals the worm, down his pants.*

MAUDE: A slap? A slap can mean so many things… A slap can mean…

DORIS: Did you try to give her one, Allarkini? One of your magic spells from below the belt?

MAUDE: Don't, Doris. What they do is their own business. A slap can mean the coldest things… But the closest too…

ALLARKINI: I wanted from her nothing…

He whispers to them, indicating the worm hidden in his pants.

… but for my worm.

DORIS: And people think I'm sick. Come on, Maude.

MAUDE: We're sorry. Terribly sorry for interrupting.

Meanwhile, ALLARKINI *and* ETHELYN *stare at* MAUDE. ETHELYN *bursts out laughing.*

MAUDE *quickly exits with* DORIS. ETHELYN *continues to laugh.*

ALLARKINI *leaves confused.* ETHELYN *continues to laugh, her laughter verges on hysterical.*

CHARLIE *speaks to* KNUCKLES *from the trapdoor.*

CHARLIE: He mustn't use that worm. He mustn't perform that act. Maude. Maude can help.

There is a clap of thunder. KNUCKLES *scurries away.* CHARLIE *closes the trapdoor and is gone.*

SCENE SIX

Some time has passed. ETHELYN *is staring into her mirror.* LONG AGO ETHELYN *look back out at her.*

LONG AGO ETHELYN: What time is it?

ETHELYN: Perhaps I should begin to pack my case.

> ETHELYN *stands in her dressing-room, putting things into a suitcase. She stops for a moment and holds one dress up. It is the same dress that came down to Violet in Act One, but it is newer and not torn now.* ETHELYN *looks at it against herself in the mirror.*
>
> LONG AGO ETHELYN *looks back at her.*
>
> *For a moment* ETHELYN *looks sad. And then she packs the dress.*
>
> *She puts the ticket into her bra.* CHARLIE *may or may not see this.*
>
> ETHELYN *stares into the mirror. She then turns and looks at* CHARLIE.

Charlie. Darling.

> CHARLIE *looks surprised that she is being soft towards him. He walks up behind her and stares over her shoulder at her in the mirror.*

CHARLIE: You forgive me?

ETHELYN: Of course.

CHARLIE: I brought you this. Happy anniversary.

> *He hands her the muddy flowers.*

ETHELYN: Thanks...

CHARLIE: You look so beautiful. Ethelyn, tonight is going to be our big night. Are you ready to wow Golden Touch Robbins?

ETHELYN: Charlie...

CHARLIE: You're what he'll fall in love with. If he falls in love with the leading lady, he'll fall in love with the show. And that's how we'll be saved. Will you be wonderful tonight, Ethelyn? Will you save the theatre with your charm?

ETHELYN: Yes. Of course, Charlie. I'll be wonderful for you.

> CHARLIE *begins to kiss her neck, looking into the mirror with her.* LONG AGO ETHELYN *looks back from the mirror, out at them. He begins to run his hands over* ETHELYN. *She sings under his dialogue.*

CHARLIE: You're still my star. Aren't you, darling?

ETHELYN: Yes, Charlie

CHARLIE: You still love it, don't you Ethelyn?
ETHELYN: Yes, Charlie
CHARLIE: Tell me you still love it.
ETHELYN: Yes, Charlie…

> *He begins to pull her dress up. He feels for what she's hidden in her bra. She moves his hands away to another part of her.*

CHARLIE: Tell me you're a star. Tell me. Say: 'I'm a star, Charlie'.
ETHELYN: I'm a star, Charlie.

> *They face each other and embrace.* LONG AGO ETHELYN *stares out of the mirror,* CHARLIE *stares at her. And she begins to sing again.*

LONG AGO ETHELYN: If I could beat with her heart
    If I could brush her hair
    If I could dance in her feet
    If I could breathe her air
    If I could feel within my veins
    The blood I boiled for you
    I could feel your cheek on her cheek
    And I might somehow be with you…

> *Suddenly* KNUCKLES *bangs on the floor of stage—mud is coming up.* CHARLIE *pulls away from her.*

> ETHELYN *looks at him, as* CHARLIE *adjusts his clothes.*

ETHELYN: Are you finished?

> CHARLIE *looks to a part of the stage. Mud is bubbling up from beneath. And something else is in the mud. Something more solid.*

CHARLIE: I have work to do.

> LONG AGO ETHELYN *repeats a phrase from the song as* CHARLIE *leaves and* ETHELYN *is left alone.*

SCENE SEVEN

CHARLIE *is cleaning up the muddy mess.* MAUDE *approaches with* DORIS *as* CHARLIE *quickly hides what he was doing.*

MAUDE: Mr Mudd. I'm glad to see you.
CHARLIE: What is it, Maudey?

DORIS: Tell 'em, Maudey.
MAUDE: I just... I just don't think I can do my act tonight, is all.
CHARLIE: Why do you say that, Maude?
MAUDE: Well, my heart is too heavy, Mr Mudd.
CHARLIE: Maude—tonight of all nights—you must do your act—
MAUDE: If only my heart were lighter...
CHARLIE: Don't tell me... is this about a certain wizard?
MAUDE: I know what you're going to say. I know it. There's no way, no how, that I could win the heart of the Great Allarkini.
CHARLIE: Perhaps you could help him in his act?
MAUDE: In his act?
CHARLIE: Help him to see that his grotesque conjuring is what stops him from being the great magician he could be. Sometimes a man just needs... a woman's touch...
MAUDE: But, Mr Mudd... so many women must have loved him in his life. And I—what man has ever loved me?

Christen O'Leary as Maude and Jim Russell as Charlie in the 2009 Arena Theatre Company and Malthouse Theatre production of GOODBYE VAUDEVILLE CHARLIE MUDD *at the Malthouse Theatre, Melbourne. (Photo: Jeff Busby)*

CHARLIE *speaks softly* MAUDE.

CHARLIE: But you forget your father, don't you, Maude?
MAUDE: Ah, yes. But for my poor Papa.
DORIS: Who took such kindly care of you after the untimely death of your mama.
MAUDE: Ah, yes. Poor Mama.
DORIS: And didn't you both miss her so.
MAUDE: I suppose.
DORIS: And wasn't your papa a handsome man?
MAUDE: I don't quite remember.
DORIS: He looked so much younger than the other girls' papas. Far too young to be without a wife. Did he not seek out a new young wife, Maude?
MAUDE: He did. He seeked her at the market place. He seeked her at the fair. He seeked her at a dance one night, but she were never there. He'd twirl upon his own heel, he'd tip up on his toe, he'd lift his arms as though to hold a woman there, but when she didn't land in them, it became too much to bear.
DORIS: And of course, you were there.
MAUDE: Oh, each lonely footstep that came up on the stair, and he came into my room, his tears—taste like air. He called me by mother's name, kept a strong hold of my hair.
DORIS: He called you by your mother's name, but it were you who was there.
MAUDE: I have been loved by a man. Perhaps it's not hopeless. Perhaps I can win the heart of the Great Allarkini…

> MAUDE *and* DORIS *both unexpectedly hug* CHARLIE. CHARLIE *smiles.*
>
> *Just at that moment,* KNUCKLES *steals the ticket from the piano.*

CHARLIE: And do convince him to refine his act.
DORIS: Yeah, yeah, yeah.

> *Suddenly* CHARLIE *sees something which makes his smile drop. More mud is rising up.*
>
> *This time, there is cloth in it.*

CHARLIE: Off you run then, Maudey. The clock is ticking.

He pushes her along her way and walks to the mud. As though it is pulling him over.

He kneels down and lifts the garment. It is part of a costume. He calls out to the rain.

He forces the cloth and wig back down into the floor. But there is a crack of thunder and again the pouring sound of rain.

He calls out to the sky.

Enough! Enough!

SCENE EIGHT

As CHARLIE *sneaks away to deal with the mud, he signals for* KNUCKLES *to follow* ETHELYN. KNUCKLES *does this by slipping out of sight, by leaping onto the walls, by squashing under set pieces.* ETHELYN *looks around carefully, to make sure she is not being followed. She begins to sneak up to where* BONES *is. He doesn't see her. He is singing a song at his piano. A song about a white woman that he adores. She listens to him in silence.*

BONES: Coon loved a woman
          Her skin as white as snow
          And everywhere the white lady went
          The coon was sure to go
          Coon followed her to the corner
          Coon followed her to the park
          Coon followed her to the old oak tree
          And watched her silent in the dark
          Coon followed her down the swirling streets
          A-swallowing every drop of her sweet light
          Coon followed her as she lonely sang
          And wandered through the night
          He watched her in the restaurant
          In the window full of light
          He watched her eating her ice-cream
          Late into the night
          He watched her toast the waiter
          She lift her glass of wine to

> Those rosy lips, the coon
> Said, 'If only to be mine'
> Coon followed her stumbling homeward
> Coon followed her past the store
> Coon followed her to her boarding house
> And silently stood outside her door
> Coon followed her as she stepped inside
> He followed her as she climbed the stairs
> Coon scurried under her downy bed
> Now every night you'll find him there.

As soon as BONES *finishes the song,* ETHELYN *begins to softly clap.* BONES *looks up, startled.*

Miss Ethelyn. I never seen you there.

ETHELYN: Did you make up that song all by yourself, Mr Bones?

He looks down at the piano keys as he answers her.

BONES: Y'sum.

ETHELYN: Who did you write that song for, Mr Bones?

BONES: Just a song I wrote. Don't even have no name.

She leans over the piano, staring at him. His eyes remain glued to the piano keys.

ETHELYN: Mister Bones?

BONES: Y'sum.

ETHELYN: Do you think I look older?

BONES: Older than when, Miss Ethelyn?

ETHELYN: Older than before.

BONES: Hard to say. Before were such a long time ago.

ETHELYN: You know what Hugh D. Macintosh did when I refused to sing for him at his theatre? Do you know what he did, Bones?

BONES: He sent you one dozen red roses every hour on that hour, each time with a note begging you to reconsider.

ETHELYN: Yes. How many words can you read?

BONES: All up, two. Bones and Bone.

ETHELYN: I need your help, Mr Bones. Would you lie for me?

BONES: Yes, Miss Ethelyn. I would lie for you.

ETHELYN: Keep this for me. Until eight o'clock. Charlie must not know.

BONES *takes the ticket. He doesn't look at it. He hides it in his piano.*

ETHELYN *runs her hand over his piano keys, in a suggestive way, right up to where his hand rests. And she leaves.*

ALLARKINI *crosses the stage with the worm.*

SCENE NINE

CHARLIE *resurfaces from underneath the stage. He is covered in more mud. He looks as if he has seen something quite awful down beneath the theatre. He is carrying a sack with him.*
KNUCKLES *comes in as* CHARLIE *speaks.* CHARLIE *doesn't see him.*
KNUCKLES *looks concerned for his brother.*

CHARLIE: Eight o'clock. It's not the end of the night, and neither is it the beginning of the night. But somehow, it has become the only hour in my life. I wonder when it happened, when first it happened that eight o'clock was the only hour that came alive, in a day and night stretched for 24 of them. Twenty-three other hours that no longer mean a thing. They're practice. They're just collected minutes to feel before, after and in between the eight o'clocks. All those hours for the rain to fall and for the water to rise. And for us to remember—I won't remember. Only eight o'clock.

> KNUCKLES *goes over to the piano and takes the ticket from* BONES *by distracting him with the piano. (This is an act in itself.)*

SCENE TEN

KNUCKLES *goes to* CHARLIE *and presents the ticket to him.*
CHARLIE *takes the ticket from* KNUCKLES. *He looks at it.*

CHARLIE: It's a ticket, Knuckles. A ticket for tonight… [*He gestures as though to say 'Ethelyn'.*] Whose ticket is this, Knuckles… Ethelyn? She has a ticket to *SS Tivoli*.

> KNUCKLES *asks in mime: 'What is the* SS Tivoli*?'*

You know, Knuckles. You know about the *SS Tivoli*.

> KNUCKLES *mimes: 'Tell me again'.*

No, Knuckles, there isn't time now.

As CHARLIE *tells* KNUCKLES *this story, he folds the ticket into a small boat.*

I will tell you, Knuckles. I will tell you about the SS *Tivoli*. It's so hard to catch. Not because it sails so fast. But the reason is, it never docks, but at the very end. Where the piers disappear into the salt and sea. Where nothing else is coming and no-one waits for thee. Where no-one waits for any man, and nothing new begins. The *SS Tivoli* arrives only when the lights turn dim. And when it comes it takes one lucky soul, to where the next show might begin. One day, my Knuckle Knuckles, the *SS Tivoli* will sail down Swanston River. And from Swanston river take to the sea. And from the sea, it will ride from inside this forgotten cage, it will sail one name, into the sweet memory of history.

KNUCKLES *looks excited. He leaps about. He mimes: 'Can I ride on it?'*

There's only one ticket, Knuckles. There's only one ticket to ride. And that ticket must go to a very great star. One who deserves it. So she wants to leave.

CHARLIE *rips the ticket into pieces.*

But our leading lady will not be leaving us.

KNUCKLES *nods sombrely, thinking this is an instruction for him.*
KNUCKLES *exits.*

Once KNUCKLES *is gone,* CHARLIE *holds the ticket out again, whole and unripped. And puts it in his pocket.*

SCENE ELEVEN

ALLARKINI *enters. He is searching through the puddles of mud on the stage floor. He takes out the worm he found in Ethelyn's ear and speaks to it.*

ALLARKINI: Tell your friends they need not fear Allarkini. Tell them, it is Allarkini who should to fear from them. For I have known… I have known these kinds of parasites before… But when… remember magic… remember…

> MAUDE *comes in with* DORIS. *She stops still and watches him.*
>
> ALLARKINI *dangles the worm beside his ear. He listens to it, as though it has said something. He wiggles his finger at it. As though speaking back to it, with his finger.*
>
> *He waits for the worm to wiggle back.*

From where you come my heart know, but my brain will not remember…

> MAUDE *watches, entranced by him.* DORIS *coughs.* ALLARKINI *looks up at them.*

Maude. You were watching me.

MAUDE: No! No—I was—we were just passing by here, on the way to somewhere that Doris and I always go… to—

DORIS: To the lavatory to wipe our bottoms.

MAUDE: That's right—our bottoms—no—that's not where—

DORIS: Our front bottoms—

MAUDE: No—

ALLARKINI: Maude. I need to know something from your heart.

MAUDE: Anything, Allarkini.

> MAUDE *waits with great anticipation.* ALLARKINI *reaches his hand up to her face slowly, as though he were going to lay it against her cheek.* MAUDE *looks so happy that she might cry. But at the last moment,* ALLARKINI *lets the worm dangle from his hand, right in front of* MAUDE'*s face.*

ALLARKINI: I need to know what feeling come into your heart when I hold this worm beside your face?

MAUDE: I don't know if there's a feeling in my heart particularly…

> *But suddenly* MAUDE *doubles over. In a dry wretch.* DORIS *does too. And with the hand that is not inside* DORIS, MAUDE *holds onto her heart.*

Oh, take it away. Please take it away.

> ALLARKINI *puts the worm away.*

ALLARKINI: Thank you, Maude. You have confirmed my suspicions. This worm is the clue to a very terrible secret Charlie Mudd keep from us.

> MAUDE *recovers.*

MAUDE: You don't need to be so suspicious of Mr Mudd, Allarkini. He really is a good man. He only wants what's best for us. All of us. [*She gushes suddenly.*] I must say, Allarkini, I entirely admire your dedication to your art.

    ALLARKINI *and* MAUDE *look into each other's eyes for a moment.*

DORIS: Tell him, Maude.
MAUDE: But perhaps, Allarkini, you could work out a new trick for tonight—one without the worm.
ALLARKINI: Trick? You think the Great Allarkini do trick?
MAUDE: I just thought you might be better off—doing something—something that would show Golden Touch Robbins—that you could be great...
ALLARKINI: Could be...
MAUDE: Of course you're—
ALLARKINI: No. Not for talking, Maude. Allarkini care only for the food of the worm. The food of the worm!

    He exits, in a huff, following the dangling worm. A thunder clap. The sound of pouring rain. A leak springs opens and water pours onto MAUDE. *She and* DORIS *stand there, wet and alone.*

DORIS: I think that went well.

SCENE TWELVE

ETHELYN *is in her dressing-room. She is looking through her things, as she continues packing. She stops for a moment and sniffs the muddy flowers* CHARLIE *had given to her earlier as a quick-solution anniversary present. She looks at them for a long time, holding them. And then she packs them.*

She is finished packing. She decides to have one last look around the theatre and at CHARLIE. *She leaves her suitcase in her dressing-room.*

ETHELYN *watches* CHARLIE. *He is dressing for the show. She watches him lovingly. Until he turns around.*

CHARLIE: What do you want?
ETHELYN: To say good luck. Before the show.
CHARLIE: Good luck? If you have faith, then you don't need luck. But

tonight, you wish me luck. Why do you look so sad, Ethelyn?
ETHELYN: Do you ever wonder, Charlie... if we had've had children?
CHARLIE: Children? What would we have done with children?
ETHELYN: Loved them, I suppose. It just seems we gave up an awful lot, Charlie... we gave up an awful lot for very little.
CHARLIE: Ethelyn. Do you think there's some empty house out there, where you were meant to live? Some family waiting for you to come home. Hungry for dinner. Wondering where you are. No-one is waiting up for you, Ethelyn. We didn't give up anything to be here. This is all we ever were. The world is empty outside of this Castle.
ETHELYN: The Castle is empty, Charlie. Nobody sees this stage.
CHARLIE: But they will. Golden Touch Robbins is coming. Why can't you believe in me?
ETHELYN: I... I wish I had taken up Hugh D. Macintosh's offer. I wish I were at his theatre—
CHARLIE: He has Vera Pearce. Have you seen her, Ethelyn? She could be your kid sister only she looks too good to be a relation of yours.

She goes to slap him. He catches her hand. They stay like that for a moment, staring at each other in fury. And then he lets go of her hand. And she slowly takes it away.

The others are happy here.
ETHELYN: Knuckles is too simple to know where he is.

At this point MAUDE *and* DORIS *are passing.* CHARLIE *and* ETHELYN *don't see them.* MAUDE *stops and listens.*

And you call Allarkini happy? With that festering, incestuous walking wound and her slutty dummy following him around. What have I done—to be here for so long—what kind of a fool would stay here so long—?

He grabs her.

CHARLIE: Violet—stop.

She does stop. She turns around to him. There's a long silence between them. During which, MAUDE *hobbles away.*

ETHELYN: Who's Violet?
CHARLIE: I don't know.
ETHELYN: You called me Violet.

CHARLIE: I didn't.
ETHELYN: You did.
CHARLIE: It doesn't matter. All names become the same in the end.
ETHELYN: Then why do we care so much if ours are remembered?
CHARLIE: History will remember. Tonight history will remember what I have lost.

> ETHELYN *goes to touch him. He pushes her away.*

Can't you see I'm busy? Eight o'clock is coming. And so is Golden Touch Robbins.

> ETHELYN *goes to the piano. She is heartbroken.*

SCENE THIRTEEN

BONES *approaches and begins to play his piano.*

ETHELYN: Don't you get sick of this place, Bones?
BONES: But, Miss Ethelyn, we is happy here. We is safe.
ETHELYN: Happy? Safe? No-one who's safe is ever happy, Bones. And no-one who's happy is safe.
BONES: Even so, it's enough for me.
ETHELYN: You're too modest, Bones. I'm not modest. There's a certain window when one may become a star. When one may escape from the confines of whichever jailhouse mediocrity has built around them—there's a passing window—and there's bars on that window—yes, Mr Bones—there are bars on that window—but one may still leap at those bars—bruised I will leap—and I will get through that window, out to the night sky with all those other stars who were strong enough to gain a place in infinity. No matter what Charlie Mudd may or may not think of me. Do you believe I can be a star, Bones?
BONES: Of course, Miss Ethelyn.
ETHELYN: I need what you've hidden for me.
BONES: Y'sum.

> *He reaches into the piano. He cannot find it. He looks up at her.*

Miss Ethelyn… it ain't there.
ETHELYN: Of course it is.
BONES: No. Miss Ethelyn. It ain't there.

ETHELYN: I get it. I know what you want. What you've always wanted from me. Why not? I might even enjoy it.

She comes around the piano. She sits beside BONES, *next to him, on his stool. He looks panicked. He tries to play a song.*

But first, I need to know, finally, after all these years, who the man behind the make-up is.

She puts her handkerchief to his face. Begins to wipe at it. He catches her hand. And moves it gently away.

Tell me, Mr Bones. Have you ever made love to a white woman before?

She goes to kiss him. He moves his face away.

BONES: It tain't… it tain't right, Miss Ethelyn.

ETHELYN: Make love to me, Bones.

BONES: It tain't right, Miss Ethelyn. A coon like me.

ETHELYN: I know you want the leading lady.

BONES: It tain't right, Miss Ethelyn.

BONES *hangs his head and looks away.*

ETHELYN: Make love to me. I order you, coon—make love to me.

She sits on top of him. She puts his hands on her, but he pulls them away.

BONES: Miss Ethelyn—please—it tain't right.

She slaps him.

ETHELYN: Who are you? Who are you to refuse me—a star? Coon. Coon!

She grabs a mirror and shoves it into his face.

Look at you. Look at you. You're ridiculous. All the men in this theatre are ridiculous. Give it to me—give what you've hidden.

BONES: I told ya, Miss Ethelyn. I don't got it.

ETHELYN *opens the piano and rummages through it. She sees it is not there. And realises:*

ETHELYN: Charlie.

She storms out.

BONES *stays there, looking into the mirror, still holding onto Ethelyn's handkerchief.*

BONES: Only time a man sees himself is when the mirror catch him unaware. In the moment of the double take is only time when he's who's really there.

SCENE FOURTEEN

MAUDE *and* DORIS *have unpacked Ethelyn's suitcase.* MAUDE *is wearing Ethelyn's red gown. They are playing with all of Ethelyn's make-up.* MAUDE *takes a delicate spray of each of Ethelyn's perfumes.* DORIS *sprays some on her crotch.*
ETHELYN *storms through the theatre.*

ETHELYN: Charlie! Charlie!

> *She slams into her dressing-room to find* MAUDE, *at her mirror.* MAUDE *is wearing Ethelyn's red gown. It is the same gown that appeared in the end of Act One, and that* ETHELYN *had hung back up earlier.*

MAUDE: I hope you don't mind. I just wanted to see…
ETHELYN: Take it off.
MAUDE: What it felt like to be desirable woman.
ETHELYN: You're dressing up as me…
MAUDE: Do you think I look sexy… like how Allarkini thinks you look sexy?

> MAUDE *then bursts into hysterical, giggling at the word 'sexy'.*

ETHELYN: Take my dress off, Maude.
DORIS: Take it off, Maude. She's no fun.

> MAUDE *lifts the dress. She deliberately rips it as she takes it off.* DORIS *helps her.*

Oops.

> MAUDE *drops the dress on the floor. She stands on it and rubs her feet on it.* MAUDE *is wearing very sexy lingerie.*

ETHELYN: That's mine. That's all mine.
MAUDE: Doris said it would be alright to try it. I wonder if Allarkini would like it on… me? As much as he likes it on… you?
ETHELYN: It doesn't really go with the dummy.

MAUDE: Uh oh. Doris hates being called a dummy.

    DORIS *swats at* ETHELYN.

ETHELYN: Why, you little—

DORIS: If only Mr Mudd loved Ethelyn, then she wouldn't have spread herself so thin between all the other men. But no-one wants her. No-one wants her anywhere.

ETHELYN: Allarkini wants me. Isn't that why you're here, Maude? Well, it takes more than a dress. It takes more than underwear. It's something that you just don't have, Maude. Sex appeal. But for your poor papa.

    MAUDE *hangs her head. She goes into a trance-like, lullaby state.*

MAUDE: Oh, each lonely footstep that came up on the stair, and when he came through my room, his tears—taste like air. He called me by my mother's name, kept a strong hold of my hair.

ETHELYN: But it were you, not your mother who were there.

MAUDE: Perhaps it were my mother, awaken from her lair. She come to haunt the act of it, a ghost drawn to despair, perhaps it were my mother, not me who were there. If it were my mother, her ghost hand strong in mine, she lifted up my weaker wrist into which she placed a broken bottle and brought to my father's head, from my own hand, a dozen slicing times.

ETHELYN: Poor Maude. You killed the only man who will ever love you.

DORIS: There's one last thing of Ethelyn's we still have to try, Maudey.

MAUDE: What's that, Doris?

    DORIS *whispers in* MAUDE*'s ear.*

Are you sure she won't mind?

    DORIS *lunges at* ETHELYN *and pulls at her hair. And sure enough, a wig comes off, into* DORIS*'s hands. Underneath,* ETHELYN*'s hair is thin and ratty.*

ETHELYN: Give it back.

DORIS: I want to try it on first. Put it on me, Maude.

    MAUDE *puts the wig on* DORIS.

Let's go show Allarkini.

ETHELYN: Oh, no you don't.

ETHELYN *grabs for the wig. A great struggle begins.* MAUDE *and* ETHELYN *fight desperately over the wig on* DORIS*'s head.*

And then, in an instant, DORIS *comes flying off* MAUDE*'s hand.*

MAUDE*'s hand is terribly disfigured beneath the dummy. We catch only a glimpse of it as* MAUDE *hides it in her skirt.*

ETHELYN *smashes* DORIS *again and again onto the floor.*

MAUDE *tries to stop her, falls over the dummy's body, but* ETHELYN *pulls* DORIS *away and continues to smash her.*

When DORIS *is smashed to smithereens,* ETHELYN *stops. She takes off her dress. She puts on the red dress that* MAUDE *had tried on. She puts the wig back on, lopsided.*

What are you looking at, freak?

MAUDE *stares at her, dumbstruck.*

They should have taken you to a freak show—better yet—a lunatic asylum.

CHARLIE *rushes in to see what all the commotion is about. He sees what has happened.* MAUDE *is shaking.* DORIS *is destroyed. He slaps* ETHELYN *across the face.*

CHARLIE: You would do this. Right before the show. You would do this to me?

MAUDE *runs from the dressing-room.*

ETHELYN: You. You give me my ticket.

They stare at each other. Both of them realising what the other knows.

CHARLIE: I'll give it to you. After you perform.
ETHELYN: The ship will be gone. It passes here at eight o'clock.
CHARLIE: That's when the show starts. And we can't start the show without the leading lady.
ETHELYN: I'm packing my suitcase. And then you must have the ticket ready.

CHARLIE *calls out to everyone.*

CHARLIE: It's showtime! Get ready all of you—it's showtime!

Mud begins to flow into the theatre. Desperately, he tries to mop it away. As he does it, a musical reprise of the previous song, 'Why Should I Now Be Alone?' plays underneath him.

> Why should I now be alone
> I gave it my best shot I gave it everything I owned
> For strangers in the dark who know me only by my show
> Why should I now be alone…

KNUCKLES *enters and brings* CHARLIE *his hat. He goes to exit and trips on his shoe lace.* CHARLIE *ties up his lace.*

> Tonight we'll all make one last stand
> I'll play my final winning hand
> We'll have the sweetest victory
> My name will live in history
> Charlie Mudd, they'll all proclaim
> Vaudeville's most famous name
> Who took his chance and won the game
> The greatest entertainer
> That the world has ever known!
> Why should I now be alone?

Alone on the stage, CHARLIE *calls out:*

Please—one more chance—Let tonight be the night… Please…

LONG AGO ETHELYN *joins in the song for a moment. She speaks to him from the mirror.*

LONG AGO ETHELYN: Yes. Tonight is the night, Charlie Mudd.

SCENE FIFTEEN

ALLARKINI *is preparing himself. He is stroking the worm. He is oiling the Machine of Unhappy.*

ALLARKINI: Tonight, Charlie Mudd. Tonight is the night.

MAUDE *arrives to him, with her hands behind her back.*

What is it, Maude?

MAUDE: I—I would have left you alone—with the show about to begin—but Doris—Doris said she must see you—that it couldn't wait. It had to be now.

ALLARKINI: Yes, Doris?

> MAUDE *takes her hands out from behind her back. She lifts her mutilated hand which* DORIS *is usually on, and holds it and moves it as though it is speaking.*
>
> ALLARKINI *cannot hide that he is taken aback by how disfigured her hand is.*
>
> DORIS *speaks in a more on-edge voice than usual. As though she is about to break. Nastier.*

DORIS: 'Ello, Allarkini.

ALLARKINI: Good evening, Doris.

DORIS: Why'd you do it for Allarkini?

MAUDE: Oh don't, Doris. Please don't.

DORIS: And you calls yourself a man of honour.

MAUDE: He is a man of honour. He is.

DORIS: A man of honour. A man of honour. He ain't nothin', is what he is.

MAUDE: Oh, stop—stop, Doris.

DORIS: Your magic ain't even nothin' Allarkini—Oh, Allarkini the powerful magician and what trick does he do—pulls out a worm. An' you mock Harry Houdini—At least he has somethin' worthwhile to do—at least he can disappear—

MAUDE: Oh, stop it, Doris. For heaven's sake, please stop it—

DORIS: There ain't no magic in him. Only treachery. Like all of them. Only treachery.

> MAUDE *is close to hysterical as she tries to pull* DORIS/*her mutilated hand away. It seems to be working and then at the last second—*DORIS/*the mutilated hand flies at* ALLARKINI*'s face. He grabs the hand as it digs for his eyes.* MAUDE *is sobbing—trying to wretch her hand away.* ALLARKINI *holds the hand steady and looks it in where its face would be.*

ALLARKINI: Tell me, Doris. Tell me what has happened.

DORIS: As if you didn't know! Treachery! Treachery!

ALLARKINI: Maude. Tell me why Doris is so upset.

MAUDE: She heard from Ethelyn—that you—that you—love her—

DORIS: And that you 'ave 'loved' her many time. That you poked more holes than could a porcupine.

MAUDE: Oh, Allarkini. How could you?

> MAUDE *and her mutilated hand run away.* ALLARKINI *looks on the floor and sees the real* DORIS, *where she lies, broken.*

SCENE SIXTEEN

ETHELYN *and* CHARLIE *sing their big number, as* ETHELYN *packs the final items into her bag.* CHARLIE *is desperately cleaning up the mud. There is more than ever before.*

And the rain is pelting down.

ETHELYN: Oh, there were nights
    Oh, Charlie, weren't there nights?
    When every man who came
    Their eyes would gaze at me
    They'd linger longingly, those nights
    I was everyone's darling… those nights…

> *Meanwhile,* ALLARKINI *is repairing.*

> DORIS *wakes up, and speaks to him.*

DORIS: Allarkini.
ALLARKINI: Doris. You were the victim of an accident.
DORIS: I remember. Ethelyn. The things Maude thinks you done, Allarkini.
ALLARKINI: I didn't.
DORIS: I know. But Maude doesn't.
ALLARKINI: How do you know?
DORIS: How can the Great Allarkini make the love to Ethelyn when he can't make the love at all?

> CHARLIE *sings.*

CHARLIE: Yes there were nights
    Oh yes, there were those nights
    You danced in satin robes
    You sang in velvet tones
    I swear you tapped the stars, those nights
    You were everyone's darling… those nights…

> ALLARKINI *and* DORIS *speak.*

ALLARKINI: You can see… you can see Allarkini's great shame?

DORIS: I can see the Great Allarkini's shame. Tell me, Allarkini, tell me why the Great Allarkini can't fall in love.

ALLARKINI: When the midgets come to perform their tiny town. I see a land like this one. But smaller than this one. I see 30 small midgets and their manager. Mr Andreas Zeyuard. The two main midgets are Misses Anita and Paola. They seduce me. I know you can't believe it. A man my height, to be seduced by two midgets. But they had rose-coloured cheek. And they had cow-brown eyes. I think they had magic of their own. For when I lie down with them, I remember not much from before I was there. I think it's a spell they have cast. I could not read in their minds. They are hiding their spell.

    ETHELYN *sings.*

ETHELYN: Charlie, wasn't I brave?
    Charlie, did I ever cry?
    I'd never let you see the secret far behind my eyes
    Charlie, didn't I soar?
    Where other girls wouldn't go
    I did what I was made to do
    I didn't ask a thing of you
    And in the end they got me too
    I was everyone's darling those nights…

    ALLARKINI *continues his story to* DORIS.

ALLARKINI: Later that night I see the most remarkable piece of entertainment enterprise ever presented in the Commonwealth. Yes, it is something to behold. Thirty of those midgets. They move so fast. They are so small. Those midgets cast a spell over me. They know knock in my knee, because it is their eye height. They see all that's below. What we do not see. They look above too. In their tiny town, I saw Melbourne much smaller, but I felt much taller, the industry leaning below my elbow dreaming of the biggest man in all of the land. I was the strongest man in the land. When the midgets are leaving they take me in their arms and tell me yes, that my magic is strong. But should I ever, ever lie with a woman of height, then all of my powers, gone.

    MAUDE *steps out in front of them. She has heard everything.*

MAUDE: Allarkini…

    ALLARKINI *holds* DORIS *out to her.*

ALLARKINI: Doris is repair.

CHARLIE: Positions, everyone! Close the curtains! Two minutes until we open! It's our big chance.

    They all sing.

BONES: Everyone's darling is lonesome tonight
           Everyone's dancing alone
           [*Joined by* MAUDE] No-one will tell their love what's in their heart
           [*Joined by* ALLARKINI] Everyone's lying and playing their part
           [*Joined by* ETHELYN & MUDD] As they're walking away tonight
           Before they have passed out of sight
           They've already left their love broken in two
           Forgetting their darling tonight.

SCENE SEVENTEEN

The song ends. And ETHELYN *arrives onto the stage with her suitcase. The same suitcase that Violet had at the beginning of Act One.* CHARLIE *is standing there, in position for the opening number.*

ETHELYN: Give me the ticket, Charlie.

CHARLIE: No.

ETHELYN: Give it to me for all we've lost. For all we never were. Give me the ticket, Charlie.

CHARLIE: You don't really want to leave.

ETHELYN: Look at this place, Charlie. It's a wreck.

CHARLIE: No. It's a castle. That holds our dreams.

ETHELYN: My dreams have never been of any interest to you.

CHARLIE: That's not true, Ethelyn.

ETHELYN: Then give me the ticket.

CHARLIE: I can't let you go.

ETHELYN: Why?

CHARLIE: Because I love you.

ETHELYN: Because you love the show.

CHARLIE: You're both the same. The show doesn't exist without its leading lady. And, Ethelyn, its leading lady does not exist without the show. Stay with us. Just one more show…

ETHELYN: Just one more show… Your whole life has only been one short act played out, again and again. You thought the scenes in your life were leading to a finale. You thought we were all hanging on the edge of our seats—desperate with applause—

CHARLIE: Our lives are nothing—if not seen. You walk off the stage, Ethelyn, and you are nowhere.

ETHELYN: Well, I am walking out, Charlie. I don't care if I miss the end. I'm sorry for you.

CHARLIE: Don't be, Ethelyn. I'm exactly the man I want to be. I happen to like my act.

ETHELYN: I liked your act too. The first thousand times I saw it. Give me the ticket, Charlie.

> *He shakes his head.*
>
> *She leaps at him, to fight him.*
>
> *They struggle. At one point she is thrown to the floor. The mud is rising, she is kneeling in the mud. Her hands are in it. She feels something. Her face has gone white, her hands shake.*

Charlie…

CHARLIE: Don't look.

ETHELYN: What have you done?

> *She pulls up her own red dress, covered in mud and blood. She holds it in front of her. They look at each other.*

I remember…

> CHARLIE *hangs his head.*

Give me my ticket. Or I will tell them.

CHARLIE: No.

ETHELYN: I will tell them all.

> *There is the sound of the ship, still far away, but coming closer.*
>
> CHARLIE *reaches into his pocket. Slowly, shakily, he takes the ticket out. He holds it out to her.* ETHELYN *takes it. At the same time, he stabs her in the heart.*

The red curtain opens and there are all the others. CHARLIE *looks at them all. He is shocked at what he has done.*

MAUDE: Ethelyn!

ALLARKINI: Mudd... what have you done?

CHARLIE: Eight o'clock... Do the show, do the show. Welcome, yes welcome to 1914. It's great to be living here...

The others all stare back sadly at him. CHARLIE *sinks down to* ETHELYN.

Golden Touch Robbins! Help us! Help us!

CHARLIE *sits in the mud, holding* ETHELYN.

ETHELYN *looks up.*

ETHELYN: I finally made it back to Hugh D. Macintosh's theatre. Oh, the lights. And there were people everywhere, Charlie. The show had already resumed by the time I arrived. They were back from intermission. I thought one of the ticket girls would stop me when I walked in. But I was invisible, Charlie. How 'bout that? I just strolled right by them. And the wind... down the aisles... I could hear the strangest wind. But no-one else could. They didn't even look away from the stage. Not for one moment. Not to see who the strange woman was, tiptoeing by their seats in the dark. There was not a single empty seat in the whole of the theatre. So I stayed, in the aisle. And I was drawn, Charlie, by the footlights, closer and closer to the stage. I could feel the tink-tinkling of the piano. Oh, Charlie—she was beautiful. Vera Pearce. The star of the theatre. She stood above me. Right above me. On the stage. I saw her right up close, from below. I didn't know what I was and what I would never be until I saw her, Charlie. Until I saw Vera Pearce on the stage, standing over me.

ETHELYN *smiles, broken.*

MAUDE: Well, that's ridiculous, Ethelyn. Hugh D. Macintosh wanted you.

ETHELYN: Maude, you fool—I never met Hugh D. Macintosh.

MAUDE: He begged you to go to his theatre. But you turned him down flat. You told him—

ETHELYN: Maude—

MAUDE: You told him, you'd rather be the brightest star in Mudd's empty Castle, than stand on his filthy stage.
ETHELYN: I told him that?
MAUDE: You told the world that.

> ETHELYN *looks up, out into the audience.*

ETHELYN: Charlie… you did it. Look… out into the audience… They're here…

> ETHELYN *dies.*
>
> *They have been singing this underneath:*

ALL: Of all the other Ethelyns
She is the loneliest one.
MAUDE: He did it again. He killed the Ethelyn again.
DORIS: He never learns.
ALLARKINI: He's killed another Ethelyn.

> CHARLIE *looks down at himself, at* ETHELYN, *stabbed. He chants quietly.*

CHARLIE: We'll find another one.
ALLARKINI: Not over. Not over.
MAUDE: There are eyes in the dark that never close. Just as one may never turn off the stars that shine at night.
DORIS: They're still here. Applauding us. Can't you hear them? That cheeky devil in the stalls is looking right up my skirt.
BONES: The magic of the theatre will never die. So long as we feed it with our own blood—feed it with our lives—it never die.
CHARLIE: Another Ethelyn!

> VIOLET *sits up. The others do not seem to see her. Only* CHARLIE.

VIOLET: No. No more Ethelyns.
CHARLIE: Who are you?
VIOLET: I'm Violet. And it's time for me to do my act.

SCENE EIGHTEEN

The theatre is silently flooding. And with the water comes terrible sounds. Bombs, guns, television. VIOLET *speaks to* CHARLIE, *the others don't hear her.*

VIOLET: They have to disappear now. You will be my assistant, Mr Mudd.

CHARLIE *laughs.*

CHARLIE: You think they want to go? You think I make them stay here?
VIOLET: You have to help them leave. It's what's fair.
CHARLIE: Love is a haunting. The only one who can exorcise you is your own willing heart. But will my heart be willing to part with her? Never. Never. It is the very being of my heart, to beat for her. I am a man standing in the recesses, in the ruins, in the ruptures of time. I made time stand still for her. And still she will not return. Fair? Is that fair I ask you? That I should lose my place in history, that I should murder the future, that I should hover half dead in the present and still she will not return? Is the heart a fair place, Violet?

She moves over to CHARLIE. *She puts her hand on his heart.*

VIOLET: I don't think love has to be so cruel, Mr Mudd.
CHARLIE: We are all frozen here.
VIOLET: Assist me in my act. Tell them. They have to leave.

CHARLIE *looks up at the others.*

CHARLIE: You have to leave. You all have to leave now.
MAUDE: Leave?
CHARLIE: Yes. The show is over.

BONES *has already disappeared. His piano is heard, floating and tinkling in some far-off place.*

And perhaps water is beginning to come in.

MAUDE: But where to? We have nowhere to go. Doris and I have nowhere.
ALLARKINI: I am sorry to part. But the Great Allarkini must goodbye.

This takes all of MAUDE's *bravery.*

MAUDE: Take us with you?
ALLARKINI: Alas. I have the curse. You are too tall. I cannot give up my magic. But do—I am—I am not without fondness... deep fondness for you, Maude.
MAUDE: I understand. Goodbye, Allarkini.

ALLARKINI *dangles the worm closer to his ear.*

DORIS: You were right to try, Maude. I'm right proud of you, I am.
VIOLET: Help them.

CHARLIE *thinks for a moment.*

CHARLIE: What if you lay with Doris?
ALLARKINI: Doris?
DORIS & MAUDE: [*together*] Doris?
CHARLIE: She's not exactly very tall, is she?

ALLARKINI *looks at* DORIS, *seeming to examine her.*

DORIS: Bit old for me. I like 'em young.
MAUDE: For me. For me, Doris. You could be the passageway for our love.

DORIS *thinks about it.*

DORIS: Suppose I better. You probably tain't none too good at it yourself.
MAUDE: Take us with you, Allarkini.
ALLARKINI: Yes. [*He falters suddenly.*] We leave Mudd's Castle for the icebergs of Prussia.

ALLARKINI *pulls* MAUDE *and* DORIS *to him and dangles the worm one end at his ear, the other end at* MAUDE*'s.*

MAUDE: I'm sure I don't know what to do.
ALLARKINI: All you must to do is dream. The same dream as I.

As they are departing/disappearing ALLARKINI *cries out, impassioned:*

The world, he has hunted me through the tropics of Siberia. I walked to Venice. He follow close at my heel—but I am fast the runner as the wind. He follow right behind the land I run turning flat to round, he call out, 'You will never touch the moon', as I was holding up for it—grasping it—yes—in my hand! I surf the waves of the Dead Sea and he come to me heavy as the salt and sand, but I am faster still. The Great Allarkini is precious bounty. But I will never fall—I sail away again. The Great Allarkini. Down Swanston River. We will sail away—if he track me down to Prussia, he will have to come a long, long way.

MAUDE, DORIS *and* ALLARKINI *disappear.*

VIOLET: And now your brother. You'll need a prop.
CHARLIE: Knuckles. Listen carefully. Bring me my gun. Do you understand?

KNUCKLES *nods, nervous. He gets the gun.* CHARLIE *holds his hand out for the gun.*

How many bullets are there in it, Knuckles?

KNUCKLES *hands him the gun.*

One. That will do.

He clicks the gun, so that it is ready to be fired.

And now I have something for you, my brother.

KNUCKLES *looks at him, expectantly.*

Knuckles, do you remember what I've told you? That you couldn't make it out there?

KNUCKLES *nods and hangs his head.*

That you couldn't make it in the world without me.

KNUCKLES *nods.*

CHARLIE *looks as though he is going to shoot* KNUCKLES. *But instead, he holds out the ticket to the ship.*

You're going on a boat ride, Knuckles. Once you're on board the ship, you just walk around with your head high. You're the greatest talent of any of us. You're the only one, really Knuckles, who ever stood a chance out there.

The sound of a huge ship coming. It's coming down Swanston River. It's sailing, this huge ship, down the last moments of Swanston River.

KNUCKLES *goes to drag* CHARLIE *along after him.*

You have to go out there now, Knuckles. You have to go out there on your own.

KNUCKLES *realises something. He points to the gun, like a question, of 'What are you going to do with that?'*

It's to protect myself. From the world.

KNUCKLES *realises exactly what* CHARLIE *is going to do with the gun.*

KNUCKLES *shakes his head and goes to grab* CHARLIE*'s arm. When he can't pull* CHARLIE *along, he tries to pick him up.*

CHARLIE *tries to push him back, but* KNUCKLES *won't be stopped.*

Water is spurting in.

The ship is coming, closer and closer. Almost on top of them.
KNUCKLES *pulls* CHARLIE *harder. And then* CHARLIE *slaps him in the face.*

KNUCKLES *jumps back, shocked.*

KNUCKLES *shakes his head. And goes to try and pick* CHARLIE *up again.*

CHARLIE *slaps him hard in the face.*

You think I'm joking around, you halfwit?

KNUCKLES *shakes his head.*

CHARLIE*'s voice changes.*

You don't owe me anything. Get out of here.

VIOLET: It has to be now, Charlie.

CHARLIE *holds out the gun, aimed at* KNUCKLES.

CHARLIE: I know you're dumb, but are you deaf too? I said get outa here.

KNUCKLES *backs away. Heartbroken. He backs to the door.*

The sound of the ship's foghorn coming. Closer and closer, it's on top of them—it's outside the door.

CHARLIE *screams at* KNUCKLES—*holding the gun at him.*

Get out of here!

KNUCKLES *looks back one more time at* CHARLIE*. And then leaves, to board the* SS Tivoli.

SCENE NINETEEN

CHARLIE *walks around the theatre. He picks up a prop. Drops it back onto the floor. It sinks into the mud.*

He holds the gun in front of him, runs it over his costume.

He holds the gun up to his head. He's about to shoot.

VIOLET *looks up from where she lies.*

VIOLET: Don't do that, Charlie.

VIOLET *takes the Ethelyn dress off. She is wearing her*

VIOLET *clothes again.*
CHARLIE: Why shouldn't I?
VIOLET: It won't work.

> CHARLIE *shoots himself in the head. Nothing happens. He looks at* VIOLET. CHARLIE *is so sad.*

You have to let me finish my act, Charlie.
CHARLIE: There's no point. Golden Touch Robbins didn't come.
VIOLET: But you're wrong.
CHARLIE: Where? Where?! Where is he?

> *A golden coat appears.*

You?

> VIOLET *puts on the coat.*
>
> CHARLIE *looks around. He sees that he is surrounded by the bodies of his co-performers.*

VIOLET: You just have to sit. And let the world come in. It hurts at first and then your lungs relax. It's so peaceful once you stop fighting it.
CHARLIE: Miss Robbins, I've been so afraid. I'm so embarrassed of how frightened I've been of the world.
VIOLET: Don't be embarrassed, Charlie. Everyone's afraid of change. Even me. Sometimes I fall in love. Just for a moment, with a moment, and then it's gone. Eras falling in on themselves like the walls of a crumbling castle. I made that metaphor on purpose. For your benefit, because of Mudd's Castle. Sometimes I just want to cry out—be still. Be still. As I turn my back to the future, but the roaring wind and rain of progress, whips my neck back, forward from the past. So it's goodbye to Swanston River. It's goodbye to vaudeville, Charlie Mudd. You've done questionable things. But I suppose I admire a man so driven that he locks out the world that would take the air from his passion. I wish I could be more passionate about my act, Charlie.
CHARLIE: What, may I ask, Miss Robbins, is your act?
VIOLET: This:

> *The theatre disappears. Everything becomes dark.*

END OF ACT TWO

ACT THREE

SCENE ONE

Everything is dark. Except for one light which shines on a tiny replica of the theatre, underwater.

CHARLIE *and* VIOLET *look into it. It echoes a toy piano and chipmunk laughter. Far, far in space,* BONES *is playing the piano. But the sound is strange and it is though he were not there at all.*

A phone rings.

VIOLET *takes a mobile phone out of her travelling case. Her travelling case is empty apart from the mobile phone. She answers it.*

VIOLET: Hello? Yes.

> *She holds out the phone to* CHARLIE.

It's for you, Charlie Mudd.

CHARLIE: Who is it?

VIOLET: It's time. That old, inevitable bastard, time.

CHARLIE: What does he want… from me?

VIOLET: The same thing he wants from all men, Charlie, all women and all children. He wants what he's given you, back again.

> CHARLIE *understands. He takes the phone and slowly puts it to his ear. He speaks, resolutely.*

CHARLIE: Hello. This is Charlie Mudd.

> *And time, the universe and all that is beautiful and heartbreaking apocalypse, spin away for* CHARLIE.

SCENE TWO

BONES *stands up from the piano. He walks the long, slow way down to the front of the stage.*

BONES: It's not so bad really. I've ain't seen everything there is to see, but I've seen enough to know that somewhere at the end of every flood, there's land. And everyone's piling into their boats. Just like Noah did. Collecting everything they think they can't stand to lose. I'll let you in on something. I'll tell you something right from my heart. But you can't never tell no-one else. Because I'll know it were you that told. You is the only one I'm telling. Because I've seen you there. All night. In the darkest seat of the house. And I know you seen me see you. We locked eyes. One time. Two time. We locked eyes. And I trust you. This is me. These are the ten things I would pack on my ark, if I happened to be Noah: 1) My piano. 2) My foot stop-itching cream. 3) A photograph of my mama when she were young. 4) A program from Mudd's Castle. Only need one, every night were the same. 5) A can-opener. 6) Can I say a hundred and still count it for one thing? You'll let me, won't ya? One hundred tins of pineapple. 7) The kind of mirror that makes your face look long. 8) Another 100 tins of pineapple. 9) A back-up can-opener. In case the first one breaks. 10) A photograph of Ethelyn Rarity.

Ethelyn floated down Swanston River. And Swanston River, like all rivers, becomes something like the sea. And yes, she'd been dead already But it were still pretty scary for her body. You don't know what it's like, the dark rust underneath a ship. The night-time sky hitting the waves. She floated to the top of the world and up near Germany. I went almost the whole way too. Following on my silly little paddle boat. I wanted to hold her hand, though of course I couldn't reach it. I like to think it was a comfort for her though, my trying like that. And finally, when the sea split into two currents, I was in one and she was in the quicker. I could see her white, satin costume join the phosphoresce that the whales eat. And I thought to myself, she'll be alright there. I hope that's what I saw. I'm ready. For the night before tomorrow. I'm ready for today.

He begins to take his make-up off, with Ethelyn's handkerchief.
You hear it? The rain. It's stopped.

THE END

Kim Gyngell as Cleveland and Julie Forsyth as Wendy in the 2011 Melbourne Theatre Company production of Return to Earth. *(Photo: Jeff Busby)*

RETURN TO EARTH

Written by **Lally Katz**

For Lois Katz and Zrinka Lemezina

Return to Earth was first produced by the Melbourne Theatre Company at the Fairfax Theatre, Arts Centre, Melbourne on 9 November 2011, with the following cast:

ALICE	ELOISE MIGNON
WENDY	JULIE FORSYTH
CLEVELAND	KIM GYNGELL
JEANIE	ANN-LOUISE SARKS
THEO	ANTHONY AHERN
TOM	TIM ROSS
CATTA	ALLEGRA ANNETTA, TALIA CHRISTOPOULOS, MATILDA WEAVER (the children alternated between performances)
DOCTOR	KIM GYNGELL

Director, Aidan Fennessey
Assistant Director, Patrick McCarthy
Designer, Claude Marcos
Lighting Designer, Lisa Mibus
Sound Designer, Kelly Ryall

CHARACTERS

ALICE WASTER, in her early 30s
WENDY WASTER, Alice's mother, in her 60s
CLEVELAND WASTER, Alice's father, in his 60s
TOM WASTER, Alice's brother, in his early 30s
CATTA WASTER, Tom's daughter, six years old
JEANIE, Alice's old high school friend, in her early 30s
THEO, a mechanic and also a fisherman, in his early 30s
DOCTOR, middle-aged

ACKNOWLEDGMENTS

The development of *Return to Earth* supported by the RE Ross Trust Playwriting Award and Playwriting Australia.

Thank you to everyone at the Melbourne Theatre Company, Chris Mead, The RE Ross Trust, Sam Strong, Wendy Lasica, Jon Halpin, Christian Leversley, Peter Evans, Martina Murray, 45 Downstairs, the State Library of Victoria and the wonderful performers who participated in the developments of the script.

AUTHOR'S NOTE

I have always envisioned this play to be played as though it is real life, with a natural feel. I realise there are some surreal and strange things that happen in it, but I see them as being a natural part of the reality of the play.

Characters accents are mentioned in the stage directions. It is entirely up to the production if the accents are played or not. It is also entirely up to the production whether or not to use the songs mentioned in the text.

SETTING

Waster Family Home:

The Waster's (pronounced Waa-ster) home in Tathra, NSW, Australia. It is a pink, weatherboard beach house, very cheerful, with wooden floors and nice, second-hand wooden furniture. It is decorated with watercolour paintings of the sea, done by Wendy Waster, and paintings of past and departed family pets. The paintings are obviously not made by a trained artist, but they have a life and movement to them that cannot be replicated without true imagination. The porch step has four different pairs of shoes waiting out on it. Three sneakers and a pair of clogs.

    It is the prettiest home on the street, the others are all quite modern, that brown/tan '70s brick, a colour so bland that it doesn't matter what colour you paint your railings, it will still be ugly. The Waster garden is charming and filling up. There are little plants, springing with life, newly planted. In the backyard, if we see it, is a palm frond, lying on its side on the grass. Beside it, is an upstanding log, which has the snout and ears of a kangaroo. The two together look like a kangaroo, lying on its side, with its back legs curled.

The Beach:

Dead jellyfish cover the shore. No-one dares to swim, but the sea looks sensational turquoise.

The River Mouth:

Layer, upon layer of life. Picnic tables painted bright colours. Fishing boats. Young families. Gleaming sun.

The Emergency Room/Auto-repair Shop:

A green neon light, that will flicker once 'Emergency Room', flicker next 'Auto-Repair Shop' and then flicker repeat. Over and over again. One half of it is men fixing cars. The other half is a makeshift emergency room. The mechanics wear white overalls. The doctor wears a white coat. This is just down the road from the Waster family home.

ACT ONE

SCENE ONE

In the lounge room of the Waster beach house, in Tathra, NSW. The early evening. WENDY *and* CLEVELAND *are in their early 60s.* ALICE *is in her early 30s. They have the kind of American accents that are common in North Americans who have lived in Australia for years and years.* ALICE *is perhaps slightly chubby looking, as though she has the look of someone who is either in the early stages of pregnancy or who is just slightly overweight.*

WENDY: There was a horse. Wasn't that right? Hadn't you had a vision of some horse? Right? When we were driving back from—No, we were driving back from that cartoon drawing class you were doing. You told me later—straight afterwards you said—'Mom, what was that?' And I said, 'What do you mean?' I didn't see anything. I'd only seen the road. I was concentrating on driving. And you said, 'Mom, all of a sudden the only thing I could see, absolutely the only thing, was a big horse rearing up on top of a hill'. You said, 'It covered my eyes from anything else, Mom'. And I thought to myself, oh, this is the kind of vision that leads someone to choosing a destiny. I always thought that to myself—because there's that constellation. That archer in the sky, who's half horse. I think you going away all leads back to that day in the car.

ALICE: Yes. I remember that horse. I remember that, Mom.

WENDY: Do you think that was part of it? Do you think that was the beginning of you leaving? Because there's something I want to show you—I made this for you last night.

She runs out of the room and comes back in with a homemade painting of a horse rearing up.

It's sort of symbolising that everything you need now is here. Do you think seeing that horse was the start of you leaving?

ALICE: God, Mom, what I can remember… you know—I should say, what I can't remember. I mean, life, what a blur, huh Mom?

WENDY: Alice. You remember.
> *A long pause.*
>
> Do you like the picture? I mean I know it's not technically very good, but does it capture the feeling of it a bit?

ALICE: I love it, Mom.
> CLEVELAND *calls out from the kitchen.*

CLEVELAND: Fig Newton's almost on, girls!

WENDY: He's so stupid, Alice. You're gonna love him. What they do is there's two families and they're against each other of course—it's a quiz show—

CLEVELAND: Are you telling her about Fig Newton?

WENDY: Yeah, hon.

CLEVELAND: Tell her about what they say about his spray-on hair. Alice it's such a scream.

WENDY: Oh—it's hilarious, everyone teases Bertles about his hair. Everyone! The audience have signs teasing him about his toupee! Isn't that hilarious? They hold up big signs about his spray-on hair! And he jokes about it all the time. One time there was this young kid on it, and he had a big head of hair—he was like this… [*She makes a big motion around her head with her hands, as though indicating an afro.*] And Fig hated him straight away because he got to have all that hair. It was so funny. But then this kid kept getting answers wrong and Fig narrowed his eyes at him like this [*impersonating Newton, badly*] and said:

CLEVELAND: 'There's not much under that hair, is there?'

WENDY: Oh, it's so great, honey—what they do is—anyone could play—you find out how much you know about people in general really.

CLEVELAND: Mom's great at it.

WENDY: It's such fun, Alice. Fig will ask a question like, what do I do with—?

CLEVELAND: Tell her about the doggies. There's always dogs in it, Alice. Basically, everyone thinks about dogs.

ALICE: You guys must love that. You love dogs, don't you?

CLEVELAND: Oh, we loves doggies! But basically the aim of the game is to guess the answer which the most people on the survey guess. To win, you've got to imagine how the majority of people think.

ALICE: Oh, right—that's great. You would find out a lot about people, huh?
WENDY: Oh, honey, it's a scream.
CLEVELAND: It's starting, girls!

> *They go and sit with him. The first question, pre-show, is asked. 'What is the most worn animal skin?'*

WENDY: Leather.
CLEVELAND: Good guess, babe. Mom's great at this game.
ALICE: Crocodile skin.
CLEVELAND: Oooh, that's good. I'll bet that's pretty high up on there.
WENDY: Good guess, Alice. Sometimes the people make you so mad—Ostrich will be on there.
CLEVELAND: Oooh, good thinking, babe! And snakeskin. They'll have to have snakeskin.
ALICE: What about cow skin?

> CLEVELAND *and* WENDY *look a little taken aback. A momentary pause.*

WENDY: That's leather, baby.
ALICE: Oh, yeah… Sheepskin?
CLEVELAND: Good guess, Alice! She's good at this game. [*He is eating from a bowl of peanuts.*] Do you girls want some nuts?
ALICE: I don't know.
WENDY: Just have a small handful and chew them slowly.
ALICE: You're sure that's okay? How long until dinner?
WENDY: We'll start getting it ready after Fig. Do you want the nuts?
ALICE: Yes.
WENDY: Just have one small handful then and no more.
ALICE: Like this?
WENDY: Perfect.

> ALICE *starts to chew them slowly.*

ALICE: They're delicious when you chew them.

SCENE TWO

ALICE *is in the backyard. She is digging, slowly, with her hands. She is singing The Beatles' 'Ticket to Ride' softly to herself.*

WENDY *comes out.*

ALICE: Remember, Mom, that's the song that we sung to Daisy. To warn her when I was going out—and she had to wait at home. She used to get so sad when we sung that song.
WENDY: When you were going out... Honey—Alice—you're digging up the garden.
ALICE: This is where Daisy's buried, isn't it?
WENDY: You're digging up the flowers, sweetheart.
ALICE: But she's buried here. I saw a mound here.
WENDY: No, sweetheart, by the fence.
ALICE: Oh. I thought it was here.
WENDY: It was by the fence. But you have to leave her alone.
ALICE: I thought I should tell her I'm back.
WENDY: She knows. She was a very smart dog. Please don't dig my garden up, Alice.

    ALICE *looks around.*

ALICE: It's beautiful. Mom, the garden is so beautiful. It didn't used to be like this. With so many flowers. And the landscape is different.
WENDY: This is where I've been. I've spent a lot of time in here. Since you left. Come here, honey.

    ALICE *stands up and walks over to her mother.*

Run your hand over the lemon balm.

    ALICE *runs her hand over it.*

Pinch it with your fingers, at the end.

    ALICE *pinches it with her fingers.*

Now smell your fingers.

    ALICE *smells them.*

ALICE: Beautiful.
WENDY: You can use it to make tea. I'll make you some lemon balm tea.
ALICE: When?
WENDY: After dinner.
ALICE: And what now?
WENDY: Now it's dinner time. You can set the table, honey.

ALICE: Yes. With plates, right?
WENDY: That's right. And what else?
ALICE: Food?
WENDY: What do we eat the food with?
ALICE: Forks.
WENDY: That's right. Knives, forks and spoons. And sometimes the person setting the table pours everyone a drink of water. Can you do that, Alice?
ALICE: Yes. It's so lovely, Mom. Your garden. I won't dig in here. I'm sorry.

SCENE THREE

ALICE, WENDY *and* CLEVELAND *are sitting down to dinner.*

WENDY *and* CLEVELAND *are finished.* ALICE *is still very slowly eating.*

ALICE: God, I really love chewing. When you eat slow you get to know everything on your plate. It all gets a personality. Gosh, this is so good, guys.
CLEVELAND: You're doing great, sweetheart. Wow, you're really chewing everything. What a difference.
ALICE: I like it. I actually like chewing now.
WENDY: You're doing so great, Angel. Did you chew when you were gone?
ALICE: You know, I don't think I did. I think that's why I overate. I just didn't need to eat as much as I was. I mean I was exercising a lot, you'd be surprised how much I was exercising, but I wasn't exercising enough to burn off what I was eating. How long do you think it will take me to lose the weight?
WENDY: Oh, you could easily lose five kilos in a month, six weeks maybe.
CLEVELAND: It's probably mostly bloat.
WENDY: You know, Dad and I were watching this real stupid show the other day—it was so dumb—it was hilarious—it was all these real fat people and they were trying to lose weight on this TV show and a real mean drill sergeant was making them do all this horrible, hard, hard stuff, like crawling through the sand on their elbows and all the poor fatsos were dyinkk—and afterwards the drill sergeant said to them…

CLEVELAND: 'Now you have to do six hours—'
WENDY: Or something insane like that—
CLEVELAND: 'Six hours of this to burn off one schnitzel.'
WENDY: And then he showed them a picture of a real beautiful, light salad. And he said:
CLEVELAND: 'This, you burn off in a half-hour brisk stroll.'
WENDY: So everyone was swearing off schnitzels. It puts it in perspective, doesn't it?
ALICE: Wow.
CLEVELAND: Mom looks great, doesn't she, Alice?
ALICE: You look so beautiful, Mom. You look like you did in the photos of you and Dad before Tommy and I were born.
WENDY: No!
ALICE: You do. You look so pretty. And so small. You look like yourself again. You didn't look like you last time I saw you.
WENDY: We've changed a lot of our habits.
CLEVELAND: We went from having these great, beautiful, big meals to these—I must say, very *langweilige* meals. That's German for boring.
ALICE: Oh, yeah. But I love tonight's dinner.
WENDY: It's very healthy. Organic.
CLEVELAND: Oh, no-one's saying it's not healthy. Just *langweilige*.
WENDY: Hey, Alice, do you love the bed?
ALICE: Yeah, it's great. I'm so comfortable.
WENDY: Oh, yay.
ALICE: You guys have done such an amazing job with the whole house. It looks so beautiful.
CLEVELAND: We knew you'd love it.
ALICE: I can't believe that you did the floors all by yourself, Dad. And that you made the curtains for every single window, Mom.
WENDY: I said to Dad, when you came back—I said to him—the first things she'll notice will be the curtains and the floors.
ALICE: They were. You guys have done such a great job.
WENDY: Do you remember what it looked like before?
ALICE: No.
WENDY: Yes you do.
ALICE: Yes. I remember.

WENDY: What a difference, huh Alice?
ALICE: Oh, a huge difference. You guys worked so hard and now you can relax. I'm so happy for you.
WENDY: Now that you're back—I mean life's so short. It seems silly for you not to be here. And it's so beautiful here. There's the beach. It's still beautiful to look at. It's as beautiful as any of those beaches you see in the calendars. Don't you think, hon?
CLEVELAND: Oh, yeah. You can't get more beautiful than Tathra. You just can't.
WENDY: Maybe as beautiful, but definitely not more beautiful. So you know you're still so welcome here, Alice.
CLEVELAND: Hey, have you talked to Tommy since you've been back?
ALICE: No, I tried to call them, but I just got his voicemail.
CLEVELAND: Let's see… They should get back tomorrow. Catta's treatment was today, so yeah, they'll definitely get back tomorrow.
WENDY: They can't wait to see you.
ALICE: I can't wait to see them.
WENDY: Catta's dying to… [*realising what she's said*] to meet you.
CLEVELAND: She can't believe all your adventures. When we've been telling her about you when you were a little girl, she sits there with these wide little eyes. Oh, Alice, she's so cute.
ALICE: Well, they've been having adventures. I can't wait to meet her.
CLEVELAND: You know she's very unwell, sweetie.
ALICE: Mom told me.
CLEVELAND: She's so brave, though. She never whinges. She hardly ever even cries.
WENDY: Oh, Alice, she's so smart. She's just dreamy. Tommy loves her so much. He's so happy you're going to finally meet her. [*Her eyes fill up with tears.*] They've been through so much, Alice.
CLEVELAND: Babe? You okay?

    WENDY *blinks back the tears.*

WENDY: Yes. I'm great.
ALICE: Do you know what's funny?
WENDY: What, baby?
CLEVELAND: What, sweetie?
ALICE: Being back here, it's like stepping back into myself.

WENDY: Everything's going to be great.
ALICE: So now that I've finished this plate, that's enough food, right?
WENDY: Yes. That's the perfect amount. It's enough to stay with you, but you certainly don't need any more.
CLEVELAND: You gonna start working it out for yourself, sweetie?
ALICE: Just let me get it right from Mom and then I'll know what to do.
CLEVELAND: Well, that's a good idea.
WENDY: Oh—Jeanie rang for you earlier today. She said she was returning your call.
ALICE: Oh… Jeanie. [*Trying to hide her anxiety*] Did she say if she was going to come by?

SCENE FOUR

It is the middle of the night. ALICE *is up, in her nightclothes. She's just sitting there.* WENDY *comes out in a nightgown.*

WENDY: Honey? Alice? Are you okay? How come you're not in bed, honey?
ALICE: Oh, yeah. I just had that nightmare I used to have. Do you remember, I used to have a nightmare where I'd be like six months pregnant, so's it was too late to do anything about it. Next thing you'd know, I'd have the baby. I kept saying, 'I knew my period was different!' And I'd start remembering all this stuff, like I'd had X-rays. For a while I used to give myself X-rays every now and then. And in my dream I remembered that—and this girl—Tammy from high school—remember she had children so young—she was the year above me. She had all these children when she was young. And she was in my dream and she came up to me and said, 'Give it up for adoption. These are the best years of your life. Have another baby later. Besides, you had those X-rays.' I said to her, 'I'm not the same age anymore that I was when I knew you in high school—'
WENDY: Well, you're still young.
ALICE: But didn't she look great! Tammy—in the dream, she'd had her teeth done. She used to have these stained front teeth and they were sort of loose from the other teeth—like wild hare teeth. But they were all fixed up now, so she could wear red lipstick and her hair was down, but very styled. And I thought, there's a woman who

knows what she's talking about. I did love my baby. It was too small to have a personality. But I kind of understood that I probably loved it. Tammy said…
WENDY: 'I'm going out. To anywhere.'
ALICE: And I said, 'I can't come. I'm stuck here now.' You remember, Mom… just how the dream went.
WENDY: Of course.

She puts her hand in ALICE'S *hair, soothingly.*

Honey. It's okay. You didn't have a baby.
ALICE: Okay. That's right.
WENDY: I don't think your name used to be Alice.
ALICE: What, Mom?
WENDY: I didn't want to say anything before, but I feel like I'm lying if I don't say. I don't think your name used to be Alice.

CLEVELAND *comes in. He's wearing his night t-shirt and y-front underwear.*

CLEVELAND: It used to be Erika.
ALICE: I didn't lie, did I? Did I lie about my name?
WENDY: No, honey. We've all started saying Alice.
ALICE: Well, maybe I should go back to Erika. Do you think I should go back to Erika?
CLEVELAND: But you're not Erika anymore. Erika always ate so fast.

SCENE FIVE

ALICE *sits on the porch step, with* JEANIE. JEANIE *is the same age as* ALICE, *but looks more like a woman. They sit under the porch light. They sit in awkward silence.*

WENDY *comes out.*

WENDY: Do you girls want some tea?
ALICE: Yes please, Mom. Can I have some chamomile tea?
WENDY: Sure, honey. Jeanie, would you like something, hon?
JEANIE: No thank you, Wendy.
WENDY: Are you sure, honey? Do you want some peppermint tea? Or do you want Dilmah? We have soy milk.

JEANIE: Oh, yes please, actually. Could I have some Dilmah tea with soy milk?
WENDY: Sure, honey. Are you girls cold out here?
JEANIE: Oh no, Wendy, it's warm. It's a beautiful night.
WENDY: Are you cold, Alice honey? Do you girls need jumpers?
ALICE: No, I'm fine, Mom.
JEANIE: I've got a cardigan right here.
WENDY: Well, come in if the mosquitoes start biting. They can get bad here, even at this time of year, I always get bitten up outside.

  WENDY *goes back inside.*

JEANIE: It's weird that your parents call you Alice now.
ALICE: Alice isn't that different a name to Erika.
JEANIE: [*counting on her fingers*] One. Two. Three. Four. Five. Yeah, they both have five letters.
ALICE: Do they? Yeah.
JEANIE: This house is beautiful. Your parents have done really well with it. I haven't been here… [*pointedly*] since they did the renovation.
ALICE: Wow… I can't believe you're married.
JEANIE: I'm not married. He's my partner.
ALICE: Wow. Do you have children?
JEANIE: No.
ALICE: Are you going to have children?
JEANIE: We're going to get a foster child.
ALICE: Right. That's the best thing to do, isn't it. Because you're helping someone.
JEANIE: I told you. I told you years ago. I can't have children.
ALICE: I know.
JEANIE: We used to talk about it all the time. [*She laughs.*] You said I could have your children. But then you didn't have any children either.
ALICE: Is it too late?
JEANIE: What?
ALICE: Would you still want to keep my baby if I had one?
JEANIE: What?
ALICE: Just say I had a baby, and it was unexpected. Just say though that maybe I'd accidentally X-rayed myself while I was pregnant.

Would you and your husband want the baby?
JEANIE: We're not married.
ALICE: That doesn't matter to me.
JEANIE: No, I'm correcting you. You have to stop calling him my husband because he's not my husband.
ALICE: Sure—sorry. Would you and he want my baby? Even if it had X-rays? Would you want it?
JEANIE: We can't talk like this anymore. We're older now. We're not—we're not close enough now to talk about that sort of thing.
ALICE: Do you see us ever being close enough again to talk like that?
JEANIE: I don't know, Alice. Why am I calling you Alice?
ALICE: It's my name now. You wouldn't have to like me. Just answer. Just tell the truth. You wouldn't have to be my friend, but would you take the baby with the X-rays?
JEANIE: Okay. Yes. I would take it. We would take it.
ALICE: Well, that's good to know.
JEANIE: That was an awful conversation.
ALICE: I think you would make a wonderful mother.
JEANIE: What?
ALICE: I think you would make the most wonderful mother. I think you'd really care.
JEANIE: Thank you.

> WENDY *comes out with their tea, on a tray.*

WENDY: Here's your chamomile, honey—it's the best evening drink. It's like organic valium. Only I'm allergic to it. And here's your Dilmah with soy milk, Jeanie honey.
JEANIE: Thanks, Wendy. I remember you've always had Dilmah.
WENDY: Oh! I love Dilmah! I only ever get Dilmah, it's the best. It really is. Let me know if you get cold, girls.

> WENDY *goes back inside. They sit there in silence for a while, sipping their tea.*

JEANIE: I couldn't believe that you were back. I couldn't believe that news.
ALICE: I was always going to come back.
JEANIE: Not to me you weren't.
ALICE: Well, I was.

JEANIE: You could have written.
ALICE: Well, no. I couldn't have.
JEANIE: You could have emailed.
ALICE: I did.
JEANIE: No you didn't.
ALICE: I tried to.
JEANIE: Sure.
ALICE: I have drafts. I have drafts of emails that bounced back. It's so hard to get a connection from where I was.
JEANIE: Fine.

They sit in silence.

God. We've aged.
ALICE: I can hardly believe it. It happened so fast.
JEANIE: Only fast to you. To me it felt slow.
ALICE: Do you remember—what's some of the fun stuff we used to do?
JEANIE: Oh, Alice, if you don't remember, don't bother—
ALICE: No, really. We had some real laughs. What were they? I treasured those laughs. I really did.
JEANIE: This is ridiculous. I'm too old to keep playing pretends with you.
ALICE: That's what we did! We played pretend. Oh, I forgot, Jeanie. We made the most beautiful worlds together.
JEANIE: You made them. I just walked through them with you.
ALICE: No. No. We made them together. Smurf Village, do you remember that? Oh—it hits me in the chest—I can see it now. You and me walking down those backtracks, but the flowers were standing out from the grey and brown that the world got painted. And we could see the colours beyond—the painted-over colours. We were giants in Smurf Village. We could see over and through everything. Everything looked so small, all the shops and the roads. Even the cars driving by were tiny like we were seeing them from above. And you said it—you said it—you said, 'Smurf Village'. And we both couldn't stop laughing. You didn't have to explain it. We knew. Because that's exactly what we were walking through. Smurf Village. We never had to explain anything to each other. That was the best part.

JEANIE: Yeah.
ALICE: You think I haven't grown up. I can see you looking at me and thinking, she's still an adolescent. You're thinking you got over all that and now you're trooping through life. But I swear, Jeanie, I'm trying to do what's right too. I might not be good at it like you are, but I'm trying.
JEANIE: Why did you come back here?
ALICE: No reason.
JEANIE: There is. There is a reason. There's always a reason with you. Wanted to make sure you weren't missing out anything, did you? And then you find out you're not, that we're all still as boring as ever. So you can disappear again and not have to wonder.
ALICE: I don't think you're *langweilige*—that's boring in German—I think you're all so beautiful.
JEANIE: So beautiful? Do you know what you sound like? I'm not quaint.
ALICE: I don't think you're quaint. [*She takes a breath.*] I need you, Jeanie.
JEANIE: Well, I don't need you anymore. Goodbye, Alice. [*She gets up to go.*] I still live in Smurf Village. And it doesn't look so small to me anymore. Maybe that's just because I shrunk too. Or maybe my eyes got better at seeing detail.
ALICE: Can I come over in a couple days, Jeanie?
JEANIE: I don't think so.

SCENE SIX

ALICE *is standing on the shore of the beach. She is staring down into the sand. A man,* THEO *is walking by.*

ALICE: Excuse me.
THEO: Yeah?
ALICE: Can you have a look at this?
THEO: The jellyfish. It's dead.
ALICE: So it is a jellyfish.
THEO: Yeah. The water's full of 'em.
ALICE: I was worried it might be a loose brain.
THEO: A human brain?

ALICE: Yes.

THEO: But look, there's two little minnows caught in it.

ALICE: Yes. That's the main reason I was worried. Man, it would be really bad for a human brain to have dead fish in it. That would be the worst way to die. I thought it was a new form of torture. But I see now how naïve I was being! Oh, that's funny! I did think it might be a jellyfish.

THEO: Well, you're safe for now.

> *He goes to walk away.*

ALICE: [*calling out after him*] I wasn't worried about my safety! It's not always me now that I'm thinking of these days. It's the brain here on the beach that I was worried about. But it's okay after all. [*She raises her voice.*] I've changed. I'm not wearing blinkers anymore. Take yours off. Look at me.

> *He turns and stares at her.*

THEO: What do you want?

ALICE: I want to watch you go fishing.

THEO: What?

ALICE: I've seen you. Every day fishing, in the white jumpsuit.

THEO: That's my work clothes. I'm a mechanic.

ALICE: You could change after work.

THEO: Why bother?

ALICE: It made me notice you.

THEO: Okay. Watch me fish.

> *He starts to walk towards the water.*

SCENE SEVEN

ALICE *is watching* THEO *cast and recast. She stares at him fascinated. She watches in utter silence. This goes on for some time. This has been going on for at least an hour. Probably more. They have not spoken. She watches his fishing as though she is watching a riveting tennis game.*

Finally he turns his head to her.

THEO: Are you taking the piss?

ALICE: No.
THEO: Are you a retard?
ALICE: No.
THEO: Are you a lesbian?
ALICE: No.

Pause, he casts.

THEO: Are you busy tonight?
ALICE: Yes.
THEO: What are you doing?
ALICE: Washing my hair.
THEO: It looks dirty.
ALICE: It is.
THEO: Will it be clean by tomorrow?
ALICE: Yes.
THEO: I've got the day off. You can come watch me do this on a small boat if you want. I go to the river mouth.
ALICE: Yes.

SCENE EIGHT

ALICE *is at home while her mother is making dinner. She sits at the counter.* WENDY *chops carrots.*

ALICE: And they were all leaving the beach, all the families, but I stayed because I was waiting for the tide... I was... waiting... for the tide to come in. Hey, Mom. I think... I've thought about it. I think I'm gonna have a baby.
WENDY: You're going to have a baby?
ALICE: Yeah. I'm gonna go on this date tomorrow with a guy I met when I was looking at jellyfish at the beach. After the families left. And I—I think we're gonna fall in love. And then I think I'm gonna have a baby. I know this is a surprise, but I saw two children today at the beach and I liked them. Because it was like looking at a photograph from a time long before now. Like they were already grown-up, but were acting out their photograph. I think that's a big part of life. So now I've thought about it and I will have some children of my own after all. I will have a baby.

CLEVELAND *comes in.*

WENDY: Well, honey, don't rush it. There's no rush. We've only just got you back. You want to be sure.

CLEVELAND: I think that it sounds like a great idea. Something to keep you here, huh sweetheart?

ALICE: Yeah.

WENDY: She should wait until she meets Catta before she makes up her mind.

CLEVELAND: Oh… good point.

ALICE: Why? Is Catta gonna scare me off having kids?

WENDY: No. Just wait. Sit over there, honey, you're blizzling where I need to chop.

ALICE: Do you want me to help with dinner, Mom? Is that what I should do?

WENDY: No, that's alright, honey. You relax.

CLEVELAND: Get her chopping, babe. It's good for the kids to help out.

WENDY: Honey, what's that shirt you're wearing?

ALICE: I found it in the shed. With some other things. I used to wear this shirt all the time. Remember, you liked it on me.

WENDY: Honey… it smells funny. Alice, there's mould in the armpits.

ALICE: Oh. I hadn't noticed.

WENDY: Honey—there's mould on the collar too. Where was it?

ALICE: Just in a box.

WENDY: Maybe you better throw it out, honey.

ALICE: But I think it might have been my favourite—

WENDY: Throw it out.

There's a knock at the door.

ALICE: I'll get it.

She goes to the door. There's JEANIE, *with a basket of fruit.*

JEANIE: Hi, Alice.

ALICE: Hi, Jeanie.

JEANIE: I brought this over for your parents.

ALICE: Thank you, Jeanie.

ALICE *takes the basket of fruit and closes the door. She goes back over to her parents.*

WENDY: What's that?
ALICE: Jeanie brought it over.
WENDY: Where did she go?
ALICE: I don't know.
WENDY: Did you invite her in?
ALICE: She didn't say she wanted to come in.
WENDY: Oh, honey! Go out and get her!
ALICE: What do I say?
WENDY: Invite her to dinner!

> ALICE *goes out on the porch.* JEANIE *is still standing there. But now she's on the step. Like she's not sure whether she should go or stay.*

ALICE: Do you want to stay for dinner?
JEANIE: I have to go home. But maybe you might want to come over sometime during the week.
ALICE: Okay. Cool. Should I call first?
JEANIE: No. Just come over. We're home in the evenings.
ALICE: Great. By the way, I've fallen in love and I'm going to start a family.
JEANIE: What?
ALICE: I'm going to be 100 per cent mom. That's my new decision. So maybe we'll take turns carpooling to crèche. Unless your foster kid is too old for crèche.
JEANIE: You've fallen in love?
ALICE: It happens to people every day. I'm one of the people it's happened to. So now I'm going to settle down and live.
JEANIE: You're a freak.
ALICE: Everything I do is wrong, huh Jeanie? Well, that's convenient, isn't it? Convenient for you! [*She pauses.*] Do you want this shirt?

> JEANIE *walks away.*

SCENE NINE

ALICE *and* THEO *are on his little rowboat, in the river mouth.*

ALICE: Big, white cruise ship coming from the end of the horizon. Whiter than the clouds. It's like colour of the foam on the sea when waves crack. This world wasn't meant to last.

THEO: Are you going to commentate the whole time?

    ALICE *thinks.*

ALICE: You, um… always come fish out here alone?
THEO: Yeah. Unless my brother's in town and we go fishing together.
ALICE: I've got a brother.
THEO: Yeah?
ALICE: He was married. He has a daughter.
THEO: My brother was married. He has a son.
ALICE: My brother and his daughter live with my parents at the moment.
THEO: My brother's son lives with my brother's ex-wife.
ALICE: My brother's daughter has a kidney disease.
THEO: I know who you mean. Little girl with the big grown-up eyes. I see them at the auto shop.
ALICE: At the auto shop?
THEO: Yeah, we building-share with the emergency room. Most of their patients are from car crashes. So the ambulance usually just tows the wreck in when they come in with the patient. We work on the car and they work on the human. That way when the patient gets better they can drive their car outta there. But yeah, I know the kid you mean.
ALICE: Well, yeah. She's my niece.
THEO: Cool.

    A long silence.

ALICE: I guess, um… Oh! There's a lot of flies out here.
THEO: Get used to 'em.
ALICE: Uh… Look at that… plant, underwater.
THEO: Seaweed.
ALICE: No. It's—I think it's a fern. Oh look, it's got a flower.
THEO: Oh, yeah. I seen them.
ALICE: What are those over there, painted bright blue?
THEO: Picnic tables. They're picnic tables.
ALICE: Do you ever…? Do you ever stop and have a picnic?
THEO: D—don't put your feet up there. That's where I gut the fish.
ALICE: Oh, I don't mind.
THEO: No, uh, it's not, uh, sanitary.
ALICE: Oh. Oh—of course—you're going to eat the fish. I'm sorry.

THEO: You didn't know.
ALICE: Um… So you hardly ever take anyone out on your boat.
THEO: Just my brother.
ALICE: And now me.
THEO: You wanted to.
ALICE: Yeah. I like it.
THEO: You like it?
ALICE: I do—I—I mean… Gosh. Sort of overwhelming. You've got the water and you can see the land—and all those trees that are vibrating with—with the wind, um—I can feel the wind—um—there's the sky up right above us. An' underneath the water there's a whole other world happening. There's a whole other world happening underneath the water. I mean there's frogs and fish an' some ducks swim underwater and birds in between the water and the grass and the sky um and they bounce from tree to tree to tree that go from the ground into the air in between the grass an' the sky and we're here right in the middle of it all. Right in the middle of it all in this boat we could come into contact—we could encounter any single one of these things. We… could kill a fish.
THEO: Well, here's hoping we do kill a fish. Or it's a wasted day.
ALICE: Well, doesn't it—doesn't it get to you? All this life… I mean—no wonder people wear sunglasses.
THEO: Why do you think I come out here every day? I come out here to sit in it. By myself every day. It's nothin' new to me.
ALICE: Does it annoy you that I—I keep talking? I haven't… God, I haven't been here for a while.
THEO: Well, it's noisier than usual. [*He's silent for a while.*] But you're pretty.
ALICE: You can still—you can still want company even though you got all this—you can still want company?
THEO: Well, it's another, it's another layer of the cake, isn't it?

> ALICE *slowly reaches across the boat and touches his shoulder.*

What's the hurry, Alice?

SCENE TEN

ALICE *comes back into the house after her fishing date. It's dark.*

ALICE: Mom?

> *A giggling sound of a little girl.* ALICE *is frightened. For a moment she thinks she is hearing herself from a lifetime ago. She touches her own face.*

Who is that?

> *The kitchen light turns on.* TOM, *her brother is standing there with,* CATTA, *his six-year-old daughter, who is grinning shyly.* CATTA *is a small six-year-old, with a pale, weak look. There is a cake next to them on the counter.* TOM, *unlike his parents and sister, has no trace of an American accent.*

TOM: Surprise, sis.
CATTA: Surprise.
TOM: Meet your niece. Catta, this is Aunty Alice.
CATTA: We made you a cake.

> ALICE, *her breath lost, bends down to look at* CATTA. *She reaches out to touch* CATTA*'s face and then stops herself.*

TOM: It's alright. She doesn't bite.

> ALICE *touches* CATTA*'s face.*

CATTA: We made a cake.
TOM: We made it with Grandma. Didn't we, Catta?
CATTA: Grandma makes the best cakes. It's pink.
ALICE: How wonderful.
CATTA: Because it's your birthday is why we made it.
ALICE: You made it for me?
TOM: Tell her the rest, Catta.
CATTA: [*shyly*] You tell her.
TOM: It's Catta's birthday too.
ALICE: We have the same birthday?
CATTA: I came then on purpose. So Daddy wouldn't be sad anymore. So he wouldn't be sad anymore on your birthday.

SCENE ELEVEN

ALICE, TOM, WENDY *and* CLEVELAND *are all sitting around the dinner table.* CATTA *is sitting on the floor playing with a doll. But she's not actually playing. She's watching* ALICE. *Everyone else has finished eating.* ALICE *is still slowly cutting, forking and chewing. She is three quarters of the way through her meal.*

WENDY: Isn't it marvellous, Tom, how slow she eats now?

TOM: Unbelievable.

WENDY: How was the drive back, honey?

TOM: Aw, unbelievable, Mum. Tell Grandma what we did when we stopped at the beach, Catta.

CATTA: I made a sandcastle. And Daddy helped me.

TOM: You made a castle for a princess, didn't you, sweet pea?

CATTA: Daddy said I could be the princess of the sandcastle.

ALICE: That's what you used to call Nadine. Princess.

> *Everyone is silent.*
>
> You would say—you would be talking—you would be saying something funny and the whole room would be laughing and she would pretend that she wasn't listening. But everyone else would be in hysterics and you'd be laughing along with the others, but your eyes would—they'd be pulled to her. My God, wasn't she—wasn't she the most beautiful girl that any of us had ever seen by then? She looked like she'd walked off the movie screen. And her clothes were perfect for her skin, but she wasn't vain. She was just sensible about it. And you, Tom—you'd be in the middle of a joke, have the whole room in the palm of your hand and you'd turn it over to her, just as you got to the punch line you'd say, 'And tell them what happened then, Princess'. And she'd roll her eyes like it was a chore, but she'd be fighting back that smile. It must have been a huge feeling, the two of you holding the whole world, palm to palm.

CATTA: Mummy.

WENDY: Pipe down, Alice.

ALICE looks confused. And then thinks of something.

ALICE: Hey, Tommy, remember this?

She picks up a bottle of soft drink—'Sunshine Pine'—off the table and stands up and starts to spin in a circle, chanting:

Sunshine Pine! Sunshine Pine! Sunshine Pine!

TOM: Yeah, I remember. [*Awkwardly*] Ha ha.

ALICE *keeps going.*

ALICE: Sunshine Pine! Sunshine Pine! Sunshine Pine! Sunshine Pine! Sunshine Pine! Remember, Tom?

TOM: Yeah, ha.

ALICE: Sunshine Pine! Sunshine Pine! Sunshine Pine—

ALICE *gets louder and louder.*

WENDY: I think she wants you to join in, sweetheart.

TOM: No. I don't want to, Mum.

WENDY: You kids used to love doing that. Remember, Cleve? We had to send their friends home.

ALICE: Sunshine Pine! Sunshine Pine! Sunshine Pine.

TOM: Sit down, Alice.

ALICE: Sunshine Pine. Sunshine Pine. Sunshine Pine.

WENDY: Just join her, Tom. Just for one round.

TOM *looks at his mother. Sighs and stands up.*

TOM: Sunshine Pine. Sunshine Pine. Sunshine Pine. Okay, let's sit down, Alice.

ALICE: Sunshine Pine! Sunshine Pine! Sunshine Pine!

TOM: You know what? Screw this. [*He walks to the door.*] Time for bed, Catta.

CATTA *goes to follow him, but then stops at the door.* ALICE *is laughing and calling out:*

ALICE: Sunshine Pine! Sunshine Pine! Sunshine Pine!

CATTA: Aunt Erika.

ALICE *stops. Looks at* CATTA.

Earth to Aunt Erika.

WENDY: Did you hear that, Cleve? Did you hear what Catta—?

CLEVELAND: She called her…

WENDY: Erika.

ALICE *stands in the middle of the room.*

SCENE TWELVE

ALICE *is standing in the living room, still. But now she is in a nightgown.* TOM *walks in on his way to the bathroom. It's late at night. Around 11 p.m.*

TOM: I'm just going to the toilet. I didn't get up to talk to you.

ALICE: Okay.

TOM: But in the future, don't bring up my wife like you ever cared about either of us. Okay?

ALICE: Okay.

TOM: And if you do bring her up then at least have the decency to keep talking about her. Don't bring my wife up and then jump off the deep end. Got it?

ALICE: Okay.

TOM: Besides, how do we even know if you're going to stay here? So don't bring up my wife again unless you plan on staying here. Unless you plan on being my sister again. Don't talk to my daughter unless you plan on being her aunt. Don't talk to Mum and Dad unless—

ALICE: Okay.

TOM: So are you going to stay here?

ALICE: I don't know, Tom.

TOM: You just passing through, huh.

ALICE: I don't know.

TOM: I need you to stay, Alice. I'm stuffed. I need you to stay.

ALICE: What do you mean?

TOM: I'm stuffed. I need you.

ALICE: If I go, Tommy, you can always come with me.

TOM: Sure. [*He takes a breath.*] I really need you, Alice... I need to ask you something—

ALICE: Do you want to go fishing on the weekend?

TOM: Fishing?

ALICE: We don't have to catch anything.

TOM: I promised Catta we'd go rollerskating. Come with us.

ALICE: I am planning to stay, Tom. I've fallen in love and I'm planning on having a baby.

TOM: [*tiredly*] Well, that's good news, Alice.

As he is leaving, ALICE *says to him, softly.*

ALICE: Tommy. I found something for you.
TOM: What?
ALICE: It was in the bottom of the medicine cabinet in the bathroom.

She takes out a make-up case.

TOM: What?
ALICE: It has her name on it.
TOM: Nadine. Her overnight cosmetic bag. Is that what it is?
ALICE: Open it up.

TOM *opens up the bag. He takes out a lipstick. He holds the lipstick up before his face.*

TOM: That's the colour… [*He starts to cry softly. He holds the lipstick closer to his face.*] That's the exact colour of her lips. [*But then he looks at the lipstick even closer.*] What's this—what's this on top—what's this growing on top—is it rotting—what is it?
ALICE: No, Tommy. It's just moss. That's all.
TOM: Moss…
ALICE: It's on the mascara brush too. Just a little bit of soft, green, gentle moss.

SCENE THIRTEEN

THEO *is fishing in his white mechanic's overalls.* ALICE *is watching him, very slowly eating a hard-boiled egg. He has eggshell all around his feet, from all the eggs he's eaten.*

THEO: Can I have some of your egg?
ALICE: Um hmm.

She walks over and hands him the rest of the egg. He puts it in his mouth, chews it, swallows it.

THEO: You want to share another one?
ALICE: Okay.

She takes another egg out. She peels the shell off. And then purposefully drops it on the sand.

THEO: Why did you do that?

ALICE: Because I love you.
THEO: Was that the last one?
ALICE: Yes.
THEO: Alright then.

He grabs her and starts to dry rut her standing up.

And then he stops just as quickly.

Satisfied?

He picks up his fishing line.

ALICE: Happy. But not satisfied.

She unzips his mechanics overalls from behind him. She starts to lower them off him. He jerks away from her.

It's okay. I know what to do.
THEO: Had a bit of practice, have you?

She tries to pull the overalls down. He pushes her down in the sand.

You want it so bad, learn how to give it to yourself.
ALICE: Don't be afraid, Theo.
THEO: I don't need anyone to get me off.

He reaches his hand into his pants. Mimics wanking, but then takes his hand back out again and starts fishing.

ALICE: You can show me everything, Theo.
THEO: I could piss on you if I wanted. I could piss on you if you don't stand up. Stand up, Alice.
ALICE: I love you, Theo.
THEO: I know and I don't like it.
ALICE: I've stopped giving myself X-rays. I want to have a baby with you.
THEO: I'm not a dolly, Alice.

He packs up his stuff, leaves. She calls out after him.

ALICE: Do you want to come rollerskating tomorrow with me and my niece?

SCENE FOURTEEN

On the driveway outside the house. CATTA *is in rollerskates. She's very wobbly at it. She doesn't have much energy.* ALICE *and* TOM *skate with her.* TOM *pulls* CATTA *along.* ALICE *is the best at skating.* TOM *is all knees.*

TOM *is speaking quickly, as though if he says it fast enough, the idea will sound flawless.* CATTA *sits down on the driveway as they talk.*

TOM: Would you be interested in that? I mean, you're a good typist. Are you still a good typist? But it would have to be something you were interested in, or there would be no point.
ALICE: Yeah, sure. If I got to work with you, that would be cool.
TOM: I mean, we couldn't hang out that much at work or anything. But we could maybe have lunch together. [*He stops for a second.*] You think I'm so boring. At least pretend you're listening, Alice.
ALICE: I am listening, Tommy. I think it's a great idea.
TOM: Really?
ALICE: Yeah.
TOM: Maybe the three of us could get a place together and get out of Mum and Dad's hair. I know they love having us, but it's a strain on them, especially with Catta being U-N-W-E-L-L...

   CATTA *looks up at her name.*

I don't know what we would have done if we weren't staying with them. I would have had to quit my job.
ALICE: But I might be getting married, Tom.
TOM: Well, as long as you've got somewhere. Either way you could come and work with me—don't you think?
ALICE: That all sounds brilliant, Tom.
TOM: I just feel like you're not listening to me seriously though, Alice.
ALICE: I'm telling you, Tom, I'm into it.
TOM: It could be like when we were kids. Only I'd be your boss. But not forever. I wouldn't be your boss forever. Someone as smart as you, you don't need training. You could just move your way up the ranks. You'd pick it up. Would you?
ALICE: Yeah, I'd pick it up.

   THEO *comes in, on rollerblades.*

THEO: They're blades. I couldn't get skates.

ALICE: You came.

TOM: So this is why you've been distracted.

ALICE: Theo, this is my brother Tom. Tom, this is my boyfriend Theo.

TOM: Yeah, Theo from the auto-repair shop. How you going? Catta, do you want to meet Aunt Alice's friend?

> CATTA *pulls herself up against the wooden fence. She leans back against it, holding herself up on it. She moves her arms above her as though she is making a snow angel. A white glow line outlines her limbs and head.*

CATTA: Listen to me?

TOM: What is it, honey?

> CATTA *begins to sing. 'Eternal Flame'. Her little voice meaning every word. It's word perfect. The way she sings has the intent and meaning of an adult, but her voice is so young. It gives her the feeling of being a child vampire, someone who has seen and experienced lifetimes, but remained naïve.*
>
> *While she sings,* THEO *takes* ALICE's *hand. He softens towards her. Like a tough guy at a roller disco when the love song plays and the mirror ball spins.*

CATTA: Say my name
Sunshine through the rain
My whole life is longing
Now come and ease the pain

> CATTA *finishes singing. The grown-ups stand in silence.* THEO *and* ALICE *holding hands. Finally,* TOM *speaks.*

TOM: I don't know how she knows the lyrics to these songs.

SCENE FIFTEEN

THEO *and* ALICE *sit on the beach. They sit side-by-side, with their backs facing the world. The sunlight falls evening yellow on their skin.* THEO *is wearing his mechanic's overalls. Their faces are close, not kissing, but as if they have been.*

ALICE *begins to gently lower* THEO's *overalls down over his arms. Down his back.*

He stiffens.

THEO: I don't know—
ALICE: [*softly*] I know.

> *She finishes pulling them down. Underneath, covering the top part of his back and shoulder blades are layer and layer, rows and rows of barnacles. Like half clam shells coming out of the flesh, like easy-to-pluck weeds.*
>
> ALICE *runs her fingertips lightly over the barnacles. He shivers.*
>
> *She fastens her thumb and forefinger to one of the barnacles and begins to gently pull.*

THEO: It will leave a barb. Unless you get it out from the root.
ALICE: It's okay.

> *One by one, she slowly begins to pull each clamshell-like barnacle out of his flesh. The shells come out surprisingly clean and whole. They leave only a bloodless slit behind.*

THEO: Are you sure…?
ALICE: I promise.

> *With all the intimacy of love making,* ALICE *continues to pull the barnacles out of* THEO*'s back.*

SCENE SIXTEEN

ALICE *arrives back home. It's late at night.* WENDY *is sitting up, doing cross-stitch.*

ALICE: You waited up for me.
WENDY: No. I just don't sleep that well at night anymore. Everyone else is asleep.
ALICE: What are you making?
WENDY: Can't you tell?
ALICE: No…
WENDY: Darn. It's a doggy. It's this doggy.

> *She holds up a missing dog poster. On the poster is a small dog, its eyes closed in the pure bliss of being patted by its owner— a girl whose face is half cut out of the photocopy of the photo.*

ALICE: Oh, yeah. I saw that picture on the telephone pole. And one in the phone box.
WENDY: Poor little doggy. Oh, I hope they find her. Look, her name's Bessie. Isn't that cute? It says 'She packed her bones and left'. Isn't that adorable? Poor family.
    ALICE *looks at the photo.*
ALICE: Poor family… Grandma… Did Grandma die?
WENDY: Yes, Alice.
ALICE: What about Dad's parents?
WENDY: Gone.
ALICE: Huh. Anyone else?
WENDY: No. Everyone else are still around. Bumbling through life. I wish you could see it through my eyes, Alice. When I was teaching. All those big, huge lives in the little bodies. Coming into class every day and bringing a whole world each. That's what school was, mixing those worlds together.
ALICE: I want to see that.
WENDY: You could study to be a teacher.
ALICE: I want to follow a person through life. Like keeping track of a racehorse. I want to bet on what they'll say in certain situations. I want them shock me, but never surprise me. I want to tune in like it's soap opera, but I get to be in the soap opera too. Like I'm really in it. Not just pretending to be in it. Like I've got real stakes too.
WENDY: But you do.
ALICE: What, Mom?
WENDY: You've got us. And Tom. And Catta.
ALICE: But you could all go on, without me. I know you could. Because you did.
WENDY: [*goes to say something*] There's something… [*Changes her mind.*] If you think I'm going to give you an excuse… If you think I'm going to excuse you, you're wrong. Just because I take you back—just because I take you back with no questions—just because I look so happy now—it doesn't mean you didn't kill me.
ALICE: You're not dead. You're just like you always were. Nothing changed.
WENDY: Look at me. I'm grey.

ALICE: You got older.
WENDY: You made me older.
ALICE: People get older. That's the thing that's so predictable.
WENDY: I had cancer.
ALICE: You had cancer?
WENDY: Everyone on our street had cancer. We were all passing each other in and out of chemo. Dad would give a slap on the back to the guy who owns the little shops, when we'd be on our way in and he'd be on his way out. The tables there were covered in piles of gardening and home improvement magazines. And advertisements for organic food stores. All us baby boomers were learning to eat organic. Our bodies are forcing us to come back to Earth. We're all returning to Earth.
ALICE: But you're not dying now. Now that you're eating organic. I think that's a great idea to eat organic. I'm glad to hear you say it. I want to know that you're taking care of yourself. I couldn't stand to think of you not here. You know that, don't you, Mom? I couldn't stand to think of you not here.
WENDY: If you go away again, you'll miss us. You'll miss the rest of this. You'll come back and I'll be buried. And Dad will be a whispering grey thing that only talks about the chores—
ALICE: He's such a character.
WENDY: But the next time you come back he'll be a different kind of character. And you will really be on the sideline of his life. Because his life will have already been lived. He'll be winding it up, just looking back through the past, talking to himself. Right now we still need you. Everyone needs to be needed. That's why you came back, baby. Oh, Alice, I understand, you think I don't, but I do. But you have to make a decision to fall in love with this world—My God, you can go anywhere, but you're not going to see anything that you can't see right here in this floor. Look down there, Alice, look at it. It's a whole universe. Dust mites warring with each other. And that piece of string—where did that come from? It could have come from Jeanie's jumper? A jumper that she bought one day with her husband—
ALICE: She's not married.
WENDY: Well, with her boyfriend on a sunny day, but she knew that she was going to need something—that a day would come in the

winter when suddenly she'd hate all her stupid coats and she'd want a jumper. So she buys one that was made in Taiwan—and it's come all the way from the fingertips of Taiwanese strangers—this string disrupting the whole world of dust mites—though I hope we don't have dust mites—yuck! But that could be what this string is.

ALICE: I know.

WENDY: And… Did Tom talk to you, Alice?

ALICE: Yes.

WENDY: But did he talk to you about Catta?

ALICE: I don't know.

WENDY: You would know if he had. So he hasn't yet.

ALICE: What?

WENDY: He'll talk to you. It's not up to me.

ALICE: Well, you should tell me now. Because you've brought it up now. So you should tell me.

WENDY: Talk to him in the morning.

ALICE: What?

WENDY: [*almost desperately*] You care. You do care. I can tell.

ALICE: Of course I do, Mom.

WENDY: Oh, Alice. You'll stay here now.

TOM *is standing in the doorway.*

TOM: Did you tell her?

WENDY: No, darling.

ALICE: What, Tom?

TOM: Okay. Catta needs a kidney. She's dying.

ALICE: She's dying?

TOM: They can't use mine. It's not a match. They can't use Mum's because of the chemo. And Dad's blood pressure is too high. [*His voice chokes.*] We thought we were going to lose her—we thought it was going to be too late and then you came back, Alice. And it must be because—it must be an omen. You've come back just at the right time to save Catta. I know it. I know it. Alice… would you have a test?

ALICE: A test for my kidney? For your daughter?

TOM: Yes. If it's a match.

WENDY: It will be a match. I know it, kids. I know it.

END OF ACT ONE

ACT TWO

SCENE ONE

CATTA *is playing with a doll on the floor in her room, in a pool of light that swims through the door. It is that same night. Very late.*
ALICE *stops in the doorway.*
CATTA *looks up at her.*

CATTA: How come you're awake, Aunt Erika?
ALICE: Talking to different people.
CATTA: To my daddy.
ALICE: Yeah. To your daddy. How come you're awake, Catta?
CATTA: Excited.
ALICE: How come?
CATTA: Because tomorrow is the day of my birthday present.
ALICE: It's a bit late. Your present.
CATTA: It's a pony ride.
ALICE: Wow. I like ponies.
CATTA: You can come. It was meant to be just me and Daddy but I don't think he likes ponies anyway. So you can come too.
ALICE: Okay.
CATTA: Sometimes ponies eat the flowers that grow in gardens and then they're naughty. Or sometimes they eat the roses, but not the thorns. And then they're clever.

> ALICE *watches* CATTA*'s hand as it sifts mesmerisingly through the doll's blond hair in the light.*

ALICE: Can I play dolly with you?
CATTA: Okay.

> ALICE *sits down with* CATTA *in the light coming through the doorway.* CATTA *holds the doll out and* ALICE *takes it.*

ALICE: What's her name?
CATTA: Nadine.
ALICE: Your mummy's name.

CATTA: Yes.
ALICE: I used to play with dolls. All by myself just like you are.
CATTA: It's more fun with a friend sometimes.

> ALICE *lifts the doll, her hand in its hair. She is drifting away to somewhere else.*

ALICE: I always liked it better by myself.
CATTA: That's because you don't know how to share.

> ALICE *snaps back out of it.*

ALICE: What? Did your daddy say that?
CATTA: No. Me. I said that to Daddy.
ALICE: That's not a very nice thing to say.
CATTA: It's not very nice not to share.

> ALICE *hands* CATTA *back her doll.*

ALICE: Goodnight.

> ALICE *walks out.* CATTA *keeps playing.*

> ALICE *comes back in.*

Hey, kid.
CATTA: Yes?
ALICE: You want my kidney?
CATTA: Yes please.
ALICE: Then don't tell me I don't know how to share.

> ALICE *leaves.*

> CATTA *stays there, playing with the doll's hair in the light.*

SCENE TWO

It is early evening. CLEVELAND *is playing with an indoor golf putting game with* CATTA *and* TOM. *They are in high spirits.*

CLEVELAND: Arggh! I can't putt today.
TOM: Yeah, you're usually so good, Dad. What do you think's gone wrong?

> CLEVELAND *stands with the club, puzzled.*

CLEVELAND: I don't know. It might be because there's a lot of pressure with you and Catta watching.

> TOM *is pissing himself laughing.*

Oh, you're taking the mickey. Really though, Tom, I've been playing good. It's not that easy in here—really—there's no wind, that's true—but I think there might be a slight slant in the floorboards.

> TOM *hugs his father, deliberately annoyingly.*

TOM: You're the one who did the floors, my little daddy.

CLEVELAND: Yeah, I ripped up the carpets, and I lacquered them. But I didn't lay them out to begin with.

TOM: Ohh, Daddy!

> *He hugs his father again, annoyingly.* CATTA *laughs.* CLEVELAND *laughs despite himself, as* TOM *bearhugs him.*

CLEVELAND: You have a putt then, Mr Bigshot.

TOM: Okay. [*He takes a putt. It misses.*] Hey, Dad, I think your floors might have a slight slant.

> CLEVELAND *laughs and they wrestle lightly.*

CATTA: Can I have a turn, Daddy?

TOM: Here you go, Princess.

> *She putts, weakly.*

CLEVELAND: Ohh, she's good.

TOM: She's very coordinated.

CLEVELAND: She is. Catta, that's good.

> CATTA *grins. But she's fading.*

> ALICE *comes in from outside.*

Was the internet up and running, sweetie?

ALICE: Yeah, I think I got ripped off, but only a little bit, Daddy. It cost $7.50 for the internet—

CLEVELAND: Seven dollars fifty? Oh well, I guess you were on for 45 minutes probably…

ALICE: Yeah, I was on for 45 minutes I guess. Maybe longer, but I gave the man $10.50 and he only gave me $2.50 back. But I mean, you know, it's 50 cents, so it's no big deal.

CLEVELAND: You shoulda just given him the ten.

ALICE: Yeah, 'cause what's the difference, it's still gonna be two coins change either way. It doesn't really make it any easier for either of us.

CLEVELAND: Yeah… that's right.

ALICE: Yeah, but I mean I think he was giving me a deal anyway because I said how much is that and he said, oh make it $7.50.

CLEVELAND: Oh, okay. So maybe you were a bit longer than 45 minutes.

TOM: Either way, it's so expensive there.

She looks at CATTA. CATTA *has silent tears streaming out of her eyes.*

ALICE: Catta's crying again, Tom.

TOM *bends down.*

TOM: Sweetheart. What's wrong?

CATTA: I don't feel good, Daddy.

TOM: You're gonna get better, Princess. Tomorrow we go to the doctor and have a meeting about how Aunt Alice is going to help you feel better again.

CATTA: Okay.

TOM: Okay. You want to be put to bed?

CATTA: No.

WENDY *calls out.*

WENDY: Fig Newton's on, gang!

They all settle down to watch the show.

TOM: You wanna sit on my lap, Princess?

CATTA: Aunt Erika. I'll sit on Aunt Erika's lap.

TOM: Ask her if it's okay—

ALICE: Yes.

CATTA *sits on* ALICE*'s lap.*

TOM: Thank you, Alice.

ALICE: For what?

TOM: Letting her sit on your lap.

But really, he means something much bigger.

WENDY: Kids—okay—the most practical shoes are…

CATTA: Rainboots.

CLEVELAND: Gumboots.

TOM: Blundstones.

ALICE: Sneakers.

The answer comes on.

WENDY: Number one, Alice!

CLEVELAND: Jeez. You really know people, Alice. Have you seen how slow she eats now, Tom?

TOM: It's a new Alice.

WENDY: Isn't it wonderful? We've got her back.

CATTA sits perched on ALICE's *lap, staring at her.* ALICE *gingerly strokes* CATTA's *back.*

SCENE THREE

Later that night, in the dark, ALICE *sits by herself playing with* CATTA's *doll in a pool of light coming from the moon outside. She speaks for the doll. The doll is having a conversation with an imaginary doctor.*

ALICE: You want to give me an X-ray, doctor? But I don't have any broken bones. I'm sure of that. I know my body good, doctor, from the inside to the out. I could follow my intestines like a maze, doctor.

In the light, she lifts the doll's hand and face so the doll is staring into its hand.

I look up at my hand close in the light, doctor, and it looks like a bone spider. A bone spider shouldn't hold any hands with people. You didn't know that I've been X-raying myself, did you, doctor? Oh, I've got messages for the world. Yes I do. I've got post-its written from here to the moon. Messages I found X-raying myself. What are some of the messages? When you hear them—when you hear them you're gonna go wild. Because they're what a heart should tell another heart. I really think—I really think I'm alive to pass on these messages from my mind and heart together to all these people on Earth. But to do that, do I have touch them? Sometimes it seems like I have to touch them with my bone spider hand. But when I touch them—I think the message gets lost.

She stays there in the pool of moonlight, playing with the doll's hair.

SCENE FOUR

The one green neon sign flashes between two different advertisements in cursive script. First 'Auto-repair Shop' and then 'Emergency Room' and then 'Auto-repair Shop' and then 'Emergency Room'. It repeats this over and over again. On one side are some automobile parts.
THEO, *in his white overalls, is greasing and fixing car parts. Whistling a lonesome cowboy song to himself as he goes about his business.*

THEO, *occasionally, and without seeming to notice that he's doing it, reaches his hand up to scratch his back. He scratches it in the place where the barnacles were pulled from.*

On the other side is a white, portable hospitable bed behind a plastic curtain.

In between the two, ALICE, TOM *and* CATTA *sit in the waiting room.* CATTA *is asleep with her head in* ALICE*'s lap.* TOM *is holding her hand.* ALICE *looks very nervous.*

THEO: Doc should only be another minute.
TOM: Thanks, Theo.
THEO: Alice, you wanta come over and see what I'm working on?
ALICE: Okay.

> *She gently moves* CATTA *onto* TOM*'s lap.*
>
> *She walks over to* THEO.

THEO: It's a carburettor, Alice. You ever seen one of these before?
ALICE: No.
THEO: They're antiques.
ALICE: Yeah?
THEO: This one is.
ALICE: What are you doing to it?
THEO: Giving it a clean. So I can hang it on display here. Boss loves 'em.

> ALICE *touches it.*

ALICE: It's beautiful.
THEO: You don't have to be polite, Alice.
ALICE: No, I think it's really nice. Look, when it's outside of the car it's a thing all by itself, but when it's in the car, it's just part of the whole bundle of the word 'car'.

THEO: Oh, I get it. Your kidney, right?
ALICE: I didn't mean my kidney…
THEO: Here comes the doc.

>   *The* DOCTOR *comes out in a white coat, which seems to match* THEO*'s white mechanic's overalls.*

You better go back into the Emergency room half.

>   ALICE *walks across the room. She sits down with* TOM *and* CATTA.

DOCTOR: The good news is, is that Alice and Catta are a match.
TOM: Oh, thank God. Thank God.
DOCTOR: But I'm afraid the transplant couldn't happen for some time.
TOM: Why?
DOCTOR: Alice, you are aware, aren't you, that you're five and a half months pregnant?
TOM: What?
DOCTOR: You did know, didn't you?

>   THEO *has stopped still. He walks over.* ALICE *stares out, into space.*

THEO: You're what?
DOCTOR: Excuse us, Theo, this is medical business.
THEO: You're what?
DOCTOR: Please leave us to speak, Theo.

>   THEO *walks back to the carburettor, looking over at* ALICE.

TOM: That's why you've come back.
ALICE: I wasn't sure. I had a hunch—but you have to believe me—I wasn't certain, Tom—Theo—I wasn't certain.
TOM: Why didn't you tell us—before—we got our hopes up—why didn't you tell us—? [*To the* DOCTOR] You can't take the kidney?
DOCTOR: No. Not until after the birth and then there will be a waiting period after that.
TOM: So how long?
DOCTOR: Tom, the detail is irrelevant.
TOM: Irrelevant…

>   TOM *looks down at* CATTA, *barely there.*

DOCTOR: Yes.

In a very little voice, CATTA *turns her head and sings, 'Every Rose Has A Thorn' by Poison.*

She finishes the song.

How does she know all the words to that song?

SCENE FIVE

THEO, *in his white mechanic's overalls, is banging on the Waster front door. He's holding a takeaway coffee from the service station in one hand. It's early in the morning. Earlier than dawn. Maybe three a.m. He itches his back. He bangs on the door.* CLEVELAND *answers.*

THEO: I need to see Alice.
CLEVELAND: Theo—it's three in the morning—is she expecting you?
THEO: She should be.
CLEVELAND: I think it might be good to come back a little later.

    ALICE *comes out in her nightgown.*

ALICE: Hi, Theo. It's okay, Dad. I'm up.

    CLEVELAND *goes back inside. It's just* THEO *and* ALICE.

THEO: I've come to take you on a fishing trip, Alice. We're gonna talk about how goddamn beautiful the world is and tell each other secrets. That sound like a nice idea, Alice? Go drift on my little boat pretending we're drifting through the world together? Ha.
ALICE: I wasn't lying to you.
THEO: Just 'cause you lie to yourself too doesn't make it the truth. What you tell yourself is your business. What you tell me is my business. You're not even here. I'm just staring at the air. Hey, look. Take a look at this, Alice.

    He pulls down his overalls, wincing. Underneath, his back is covered in puss and raw, pink flesh. Amongst the puss and pink flesh are the remaining barnacles. And there are some smaller barnacles too, which have recently started growing.

You left the barbs.
ALICE: I can get them.
THEO: Don't you touch.
ALICE: I can dig those little ones out.

THEO: Don't you touch.
ALICE: I'm gonna love you forever.
THEO: No you're not.
ALICE: I am.
THEO: Don't you touch.
ALICE: I can get those little ones out, Theo. I've got long fingernails.
THEO: No. Your hands are too dirty.

> *She goes to touch him, he pushes her away. She lets herself collapse down onto the lawn.*

ALICE: You could piss on me here. [*She looks around at the morning.*] God, Theo. I forgot how beautiful the morning is. How beautiful the morning is mixed in the sea. This big, old, dead sea.

SCENE SIX

JEANIE *knocks on the Waster family home door.* ALICE *opens it and steps outside onto the porch. She closes it behind her.* JEANIE *already looks impatient.*

JEANIE: Okay, I'm here. What?
ALICE: We need to be quiet.
JEANIE: Fine.
ALICE: Have you got your foster child yet?
JEANIE: No. There are complications. As always. Is that all you wanted to know, because I've got stuff to do.
ALICE: I can't give Catta my kidney.
JEANIE: Why?
ALICE: Because I'm pregnant.
JEANIE: You are then.
ALICE: Yes. I don't want a baby.
JEANIE: I thought you were desperate to be 'Mom'.
ALICE: I thought I could live here. I thought I could live back here. I thought I could fall in love and do what you do and be a good person—
JEANIE: Do what I do? What exactly is it you think I do?
ALICE: You're part of the world.
JEANIE: So are you, Alice. Whether you like it or not.
ALICE: Jeanie—the whole reason I came back—the only reason I came

back initially—was to see you. And then I got caught up in things again. I was taken with the beauty of normality. You know? I was taken with all the dramas of everyday life. I told myself I could drop back in. That I could be someone to love and I could love too—but I can't, Jeanie. And I can't keep taking love. So I'm going to do the best thing and I'm going to leave. The only reason I came here in the first place was to see you—

JEANIE: Why?

ALICE: I wanted to ask you… will you take my baby?

JEANIE: Are you for real?

ALICE: Yes.

JEANIE: Adopt it?

ALICE: Yes.

JEANIE: Forever?

ALICE: Yes. It will be your baby forever. And you don't ever even have to tell it about me. In fact don't. I don't want it to know. I don't want any thoughts pulling on me where I'm going.

JEANIE: When is it due?

ALICE: Just before Christmas.

JEANIE: I'd have a baby at Christmas time… How would I know you wouldn't change your mind?

ALICE: I wouldn't. I'll sign anything. I just need to leave here.

JEANIE: We've wanted a child for so long.

ALICE: Will you take it, Jeanie?

Tears come into JEANIE*'s eyes.*

JEANIE: No.

ALICE: But why?

JEANIE: Just no.

ALICE: I can't be stuck here, Jeanie. We promised when we were kids—

JEANIE: But I'm not a kid anymore, Alice. And neither are you.

SCENE SEVEN

The neon light flashes 'Auto-repair Shop' and then 'Emergency Room'. CATTA *is lying on her side in a white hospital gown, on the hospital bed. There are two wires attached to her temples. The wires run onto a machine. She is not conscious.*

TOM *stands next to the bed, holding* CATTA*'s hand. He is whispering over and over again: 'It's okay, Catta. It's okay, baby. It's okay, Catta. It's okay, baby.'*

WENDY *and* CLEVELAND *stand on the other side of the bed.*

THEO *is on the other side of the room, in the 'Auto-repair Shop' part, slowly cleaning a car part.*

ALICE, *looking truly pregnant, stands away from the bed, looking on.*

CATTA *begins to weep, to cry her heart out in her sleep.*

TOM: Oh, baby. Oh, Catta. It's okay, baby.
WENDY: But that's a good sign, isn't it—that's good sign that she's crying? It means she's getting more strength…
TOM: It's her organs shutting down, Mum.
WENDY: Oh, Tommy honey.

>WENDY *reaches to* TOM, *but he stiffens away.*

>*The* DOCTOR *comes and stands by the end of the bed, with his stethoscope on.* ALICE *wobbles over to him. She clings onto his arm.*

ALICE: Can't you do something, doctor? Now is when you should be doing something. While she's still here. While she's still in the room with us. Can't you do something? She's my brother's baby. Don't let someone else he loves disappear—while she's still in the room—don't let her out of this room. It's your job to keep her in this room.

>*The* DOCTOR *stands at the end of the bed.* THEO *watches from his car work.* CATTA *weeps silently.* TOM *holds her hand.*

>ALICE *looks on panicked—hopelessly—and then she begins to sing 'Eternal Flame'. After a little while, the rest of the family join in.*

END OF ACT TWO

ACT THREE

SCENE ONE

It is Christmas time. The Waster family are watching TV. WENDY *is doing cross-stitch.* CLEVELAND *is eating peanuts.* TOM *is staring straight ahead at the TV.* ALICE *is sitting on a chair, holding her baby.*

WENDY: Okay—okay—kids—

> *The question is: 'What is the most common Christmas gift a father can expect to receive?'*

CLEVELAND: Now—this is the last thing I want, but I'm gonna guess a necktie.
WENDY: Sporting goods.
ALICE: Golf clubs.
TOM: A drawing.
CLEVELAND: Now, you kiddies pay close attention to these answers, you might get some good ideas.
WENDY: Oh, darn—the pasta—
CLEVELAND: I'll get it, babe.
WENDY: It's okay, hon. We're taping Fig anyway.
ALICE: I'll get the pasta, Mom.
WENDY: I'll get it, you character.

> WENDY *goes into the kitchen.*

ALICE: I'll come with you.

> ALICE *gets up.*

TOM: You want me to hold Nadine?
ALICE: I'll take her, she needs milk. I'm gonna take her for a walk after dinner if you want.
TOM: Sure.
CLEVELAND: Oh, man! None of us covered tools! That'll be first.

> ALICE *joins her mother in the kitchen.*
> *She begins to breastfeed the baby, Nadine.*

WENDY: It's just going to be a simple dinner tonight and tomorrow and then we'll have a real big meal on Christmas.
ALICE: That sounds great, Mom.
WENDY: Is your nipple okay?
ALICE: Yeah. It's feeling way better.
WENDY: She's a hungry baby. Just like you were.
ALICE: Yeah.
WENDY: Remember to keep eating slow. It's the best way to lose the weight.
ALICE: Yeah. But I get so hungry.
WENDY: Well, you have to eat enough, especially while you're breastfeeding. But you don't need to eat as much as you did while you were pregnant.
ALICE: It's kind of a shame. It's fun eating for two.
WENDY: Oh, yeah.
ALICE: Do you want me to set the table?
WENDY: No, hon, we'll do it in a minute. Sit down while you're breastfeeding. [*She peeks at Nadine.*] She's the sweetest thing. Are you happy, Alice?
ALICE: Yeah, Mom.
WENDY: I'm so glad, sweetheart. [*She goes back to preparing dinner. And then looks up.*] Alice?
ALICE: Yeah, Mom?
WENDY: What was it like? What did you see out there? In outer space?

ALICE *looks taken aback at first. But then her eyes dream over.*

ALICE: Oh, Mom. I mean, man, I saw stuff like—nobody'd believe you know like—trails of airplane fire mixed in with daisies spinning round comets. I mean, oh man, Mom, I saw clouds with rings of Saturn. I saw Pluto following my tail like a little pet dog. Oh man, Mom. I saw upside down trees. I saw stars up real close. I passed that archer—you know, that half-horse constellation, it was on a hill of meteorites, rearing up and then grazing by my side. I saw sand at the bottom of my ship. And the bottom of my ship, Mom, was like the bottom of the sea. Oh, when it got dark out, in outer space, Mom, well all the eyes would start shining. All the eyes would start glistening, like, hello. It's okay. We can see you, man. Oh man,

Mom. It was like uh—stalactites and uh—stalagmites. Like the uh—headlights, of a big safe car coming down the hill to pick me up, Mom. Oh, I was never scared. I knew exactly—I knew exactly where I was meant to be heading... There were... sparks like, a uh, a uh trail like. Oh man, Mom, there was a trail for me to follow. Everywhere I went, all I had to do was uh adjust the particulars of my eyes, Mom. All I had to do was adjust the particulars of my eyes, Mom. And, oh man, I could see. I could see just where I needed to go.

WENDY: Did any of it look like home?

ALICE: Well, it's funny, Mom. Because do you know what the prettiest part of outer space was, Mama?

WENDY: What, baby?

ALICE: There was one little part of the solar system which looked almost... almost... as pretty as your garden.

THE END